Improving Memory
through Creativity

of related interest

Creativity and Communication in Persons with Dementia
A Practical Guide
John Killick and Claire Craig
ISBN 978 1 84905 113 2
eISBN 978 0 85700 301 0

Art Therapy and Creative Coping Techniques for Older Adults
Susan I. Buchalter
ISBN 978 1 84905 830 8
eISBN 978 0 85700 309 6

End of Life Care
A Guide for Therapists, Artists and Arts Therapists
Nigel Hartley
Foreword by Dame Barbara Monroe
ISBN 978 1 84905 133 0
eISBN 978 0 85700 336 2

The Creative Arts in Dementia Care
Practical Person-Centred Approaches and Ideas
Jill Hayes
With Sarah Povey
Foreword by Shaun McNiff
ISBN 978 1 84905 056 2
eISBN 978 0 85700 251 8

Neuroscience for Counsellors
Practical Applications for Counsellors, Therapists and Mental Health
Rachal Zara Wilson
ISBN 978 1 84905 488 1
eISBN 978 0 85700 894 7

Improving Memory
through Creativity

*A Professional's Guide to Culturally Sensitive
Cognitive Training with Older Adults*

AMANDA ALDERS PIKE

Jessica Kingsley *Publishers*
London and Philadelphia

First published in 2014
by Jessica Kingsley Publishers
73 Collier Street
London N1 9BE, UK
and
400 Market Street, Suite 400
Philadelphia, PA 19106, USA

www.jkp.com

Library of Congress Cataloging in Publication Data
Pike, Amanda, author.
  Improving memory through creativity : a professional's guide to culturally-sensitive
cognitive training
with older adults / Amanda Pike.
       p. ; cm.
  Includes bibliographical references and index.
  ISBN 978-1-84905-953-4 (alk. paper)
  I. Title.
  [DNLM: 1. Memory Disorders--rehabilitation. 2. Aged. 3. Art Therapy--methods.
4. Cognitive Therapy-
-methods. 5. Creativity. 6. Cultural Competency. WM 173.7]
  RC394.M46
  616.8'3--dc23
                            2013031647

British Library Cataloguing in Publication Data
A CIP catalogue record for this book is available from the British Library

ISBN 978 1 84905 953 4
eISBN 978 0 85700 809 1

Printed and bound by Bell & Bain Ltd, Glasgow

This book is dedicated to my family. Also, this book is dedicated to the older adults and caregivers who have and hopefully will continue to benefit from these techniques.

ACKNOWLEDGEMENT

I would like to thank Erika Deoudes for tirelessly working on the illustrations contained within this book and for assisting in editing.

CONTENTS

PREFACE.   11

1 Late-Life Creative Self-Expression and Memory   13
   Creativity for enhanced cognitive performance   14
   How to apply information presented within this text   15
   Normal and abnormal aging   19
   Alzheimer's disease   20
   Risk factors of memory loss.   21
   Self-expression in late-life   24
   Encouraging mental stimulation through expressive art-making   27
   Incorporating creativity into older adult identity through
        art-making.   28
   Summary   38

2 Happiness, Social Creativity, and the Brain   39
   Happiness and creative self-expression   40
   Happiness, creativity, and the brain   44
   Neurotransmitters and creativity   47
   Making art that expresses and enhances mood   53
   Combining visual elements for enhanced mood   58
   Social equality vs. stratification during creativity and happiness   61
   Summary   63

3 Culture, Communication, and Art.   64
   Promoting socialization during memory training   64
   Culture.   66
   Communication   72

Visual literacy. 77

Social sharing of meaning through art 78

Summary 82

4 Cognitive Training through Creative Self-expression .   83

Addressing cognitive abilities. 83

Emotion-focused interventions 85

Nature of cognitive impairment. 87

Type of memory impacted. 93

Cognitive training 94

Expressivity-based memory techniques 97

Neurobiology of creativity and expressivity. 102

Theory: going beyond "recipes". 103

Educational vs. therapeutic frameworks. 108

Summary 112

5 Using Art to Understanrd the Mind   113

Elements of successful sessions 114

Additional planning for effective sessions 116

Rhythmic structure and versatility in directives. 118

Outline of ten weeks of sessions 120

A single directive for all ten weeks 129

Concluding the ten weeks 133

Summary 134

6 Going Beyond the Book: Community Collaborations   135

Scope-of-practice. 136

Cultural trends in seeking care. 138

Caregivers 139

Inter-generational projects 140

Services/systems of care across settings. 142

Getting started. 147

Identifying symptoms cross-culturally 152

Organizations. 158

Ways to continue learning 161

Additional resources and references. 161

Summary 162

References 169

Subject Index 182

Author Index 189

LIST OF TABLES

Table 1.1 Domains and artistic creativity 16

Table 1.2 Goals: memory training through creative
self-expression 19

Table 1.3 Steps to elicit creative behavior 29

Table 1.4 Steps for encouraging confident creative thinking . . . 32

Table 1.5 Concepts related to creative self-expression 36

Table 2.1 Categories of positive emotion and creative
experience 42

Table 2.2 Neurotransmitters, brain waves, and
memory training 48

Table 2.3 Serotonin and creativity 49

Table 2.4 Dopamine and creativity 51

Table 2.5 Acetylcholine and creativity 53

Table 2.6 Line type, associations, effect 57

Table 2.7 Space occupied, associations, effect 58

Table 3.1 Idiomatic equivalents 74

Table 4.1 Overview of parallels between CT and
artistic creativity 98

Table 4.2 Examples of art session content 101

Table 4.3 Theories that may guide creativity-based
memory training 108

Table 5.1 Example session plans 115

Table 5.2 Timeline example for a session 116

Table 5.3 Examples of openings and closings 118

Table 5.4 Week one and two: Kinesthetic/Sensory level
(2 sessions/2 directives) 122

Table 5.5 Week three and four: Perceptive/Affective level
(2 sessions/2 directives) 123

Table 5.6 Week five and six: Cognitive/Symbolic level
(2 sessions/2 directives) 125

Table 5.7 Week seven and eight: Perceptive/Affective level . . . 127

Table 5.8 Week nine and ten: Kinesthetic/Symbolic level 128

Table 6.1 Topics to engage the family 141

Table 6.2 Family inclusive directives 142

Table 6.3 Facilities where creative professionals work with
older adults 146

Table 6.4 Organizational resources 159

LIST OF FIGURES

Figure 1.1 Hippocampus in the brain 20

Figure 2.1 Rorschach blot done with paint on folded paper . . . 42

Figure 2.2 Neurons firing 45

Figure 2.3 Unstable vs. stable firing 45

Figure 2.4 Comparison between ocean waves and brain waves 46

Figure 2.5 Mandala 49

Figure 2.6 Quadrants 60

Figure 3.1 Model of social inclusivity by hierarchies 69

Figure 3.2 Art as the center of the social process 70

Figure 3.3 Triadic schema 76

Figure 4.1 Foreground, middle-ground, and background 90

Figure 4.2 Cortical thickness 102

Figure 4.3 Kinesthetic/Sensory (K/S) level artwork 106

Figure 4.4 Perceptual/Affective (P/A) level artwork 106

Figure 4.5 Cognitive/Symbolic (C/Sy) level artwork 107

Figure 4.6 Linear model of increasing difficulty 109

Figure 4.7 Self-report of memory 110

Figure 4.8 Therapeutic memory training framework 111

Figure 4.9 Optimal pattern of long-term stimulation 112

Figure 6.1 Session in partnership with a yoga studio 144

Figure 6.2 Brain atrophy and CDT score 154

Figure 6.3 "M": pre-test score: 4 out of 10; post-test: 5
out of 10 155

Figure 6.4 "R": pre-test score: 4.3 out of 10; post-test: 7.3
out of 10 155

Figure 6.5 "J": pre-test score: 1.7 out of 10; post-test: 7.7
out of 10 155

Figure 6.6 Graphic indicators of impairment 157

PREFACE

Before I began my work as a therapist, I worked internationally as an artist, exhibiting, painting portraits, and doing murals. As a result, my area of expertise is related to the visual arts. Currently, I am an art therapist, which means that I hold a Master's degree with a specialization in art therapy; my doctorate also reflects this specialization. Even though I believe that older adults can benefit from a wide range of expressivity—from music to dance to drama—the content of this book stems from my own clinical experiences, and the exercises herein are rooted in visual expressivity.

My intention in writing this guidebook is to present established scientific findings as well as my own research and experiences. My doctoral research focused on how art therapy affects cognitive performance among ethnically diverse older adults. However, in writing this book, I aim to present my findings in ways that appeal to a wide variety of professionals.

My hope is that the neuroscience concepts presented will be easily understood. I prioritized including only a few neuroscientific concepts related to creativity, aging, and cognitive training. In doing so, I aim to keep the information relevant and accessible to creative professionals and not to overwhelm the reader.

Studies relating to the brain, older adults, memory, and cognitive training are rapidly increasing. However, the older adult population within the US is diverse in both culture and ethnicity, and this is a distinction which is rarely addressed. In writing this book, I hope to provide information that is currently not available for professionals. This book is descriptive in nature and illustrates how cognitive training may naturally be incorporated into creative sessions.

There is a growing need for culturally sensitive techniques, which can be applied by professionals with a variety of backgrounds. Because art therapy is a relatively small field, I expect that many of those reading this book will not be art therapists. For that reason, my focus is on instilling knowledge that many different professionals can use to benefit diverse older adults. Although I will draw from art therapy theories, the structure that I propose aligns with cognitive training and is, therefore, versatile. That said, the theories presented are related to a mental healthcare background and for that reason I ask the reader to closely consider the scope-of-practice and the referral information presented in Chapter 6.

Please note that the session content that I outline throughout this book cannot ethically be called "therapy" (but can absolutely be called "therapeutic") unless the sessions are performed by an individual with a Master's degree in a mental health related field (e.g. art therapy, counseling, social work). Additionally, the use of the title "art therapist" and the description of sessions as art therapy are terms normally reserved for persons who hold a Master's degree in art therapy.

Collaboration among professionals benefits everyone involved. I would be very happy to work with anyone interested in a research partnership. I am also able to provide supervision for those seeking art therapy credentials or to provide consultation regarding art therapy, including outcome study consultation. To contact me, please visit my website at www.arttherapyconsulting.com

LATE-LIFE CREATIVE SELF-EXPRESSION AND MEMORY

KEY CONCEPT: Alzheimer's disease and debilitating memory loss are not a normal part of aging.

WORDBANK
(Definitions can be found throughout the chapter.)

1	Alzheimer's disease	9	Involuntary memories
2	Mild cognitive impairment	10	Cortisol
3	Neuroplasticity	11	Neurogenesis
4	Creative self-expression	12	Meaning
5	Gero-expressivity	13	Aesthetic experience
6	Cognitive training	14	Ageism
7	Enriched environment	15	Artistic creativity
8	Hippocampus	16	Art

Aging is the core issue of our time, and society is depending on new and innovative strategies to address the health and psychosocial factors associated with aging. Older adults will soon outnumber younger generations, and as the older adult population rises, so too do health concerns such as cognitive impairment and Alzheimer's disease (Larrieu *et al.* 2002). Older adults come from many different cultural and ethnic backgrounds and their needs are as varied as their cultural practices. Society can no longer afford to be satisfied with simplistic and narrow views about aging and older adult needs. Strategies that are culturally inclusive are in high demand.

Specifically, there is a critical need to ensure the mental abilities of older adults from all cultural backgrounds so they can continue to be independent, contributing members of society. Throughout this book, I propose artistic creativity as one culturally inclusive strategy for addressing the cognitive needs of diverse older adults. Art is broadly cognitive, and the capacity to experience enrichment from viewing and/or making a work of art is universal (Brinck 2007). Unlike other interventions that aim to stimulate cognition, art images exist in all cultures and do not require a specific reading level or certain levels of previous education to engage mental faculties (Morris and Stuhr 2001). When viewing art, complexity, novelty, and uncertainty provoke memory and association (Epstein 1991). When viewing artwork, either during the process of making it or once it is completed, older adults can use their personal and cultural experiences to make sense of it and this is a form of mental stimulation.

Before 1960, the brain was considered immutable and incapable of new cell growth. However, by 1964, researchers realized that the brain positively responds, adapts, and changes with stimulation and experience (Mungas *et al.* 2009). A growing body of research suggests that active mental stimulation such as through cognitive training may promote improved cognition and inhibit age-related cognitive decline (Willis *et al.* 2006). Cognitive training, also called memory training, is an umbrella term for interventions aimed at improving such abilities as attention, memory, reasoning, problem solving, and decision making (Sitzer, Twamley, and Jeste 2006). Mental stimulation, such as through cognitive training coupled with positive emotional and social experiences, promotes optimal brain states in older adults (Davidson 2003; Glei *et al.* 2005).

Creativity for enhanced cognitive performance

Thinking and remembering are largely based on mental images, and art-making incorporates these mental images thereby stimulating memory recall. Selective visualization and mental imagery are central to memory, and much of cognitive functioning depends on one's ability to visualize (Vanlierde and Wanet-Defalque 2005). Artistic creativity involves visualization and incorporates two processes: thinking and producing (Cohen 2006; Weisberg 2010). Art-making is a complex process of representing, organizing, and interpreting mental imagery and involves diverse neural connections throughout the brain (Mendez 2004). Through encouragement, training, and motivated practice, creativity can be developed; it does not require inborn talent (Naiman 2011). Prior education and ability in art-making are not necessary for older adults to experience the benefits associated with art-making (Cummings *et al.* 2008).

Creativity is mentally stimulating as well as emotionally and socially gratifying. This combination promotes optimal brain wellness and can improve memory, especially when used in combination with cognitive training strategies (Alders 2012). In this book, I will describe how memory skills can be targeted for improvement through creative self-expression. When older adults are encouraged to self-express, creativity will naturally arise. Through creativity, the older adult will have the opportunity for enhanced cognitive performance, which leads to improved memory skills.

Throughout this book, I will provide information on how creative self-expression can help older adults maintain and improve their existing cognitive abilities. I will outline research that describes how and why a combination of positive emotions, dynamic interaction, and mental stimulation all contribute to optimal brain functioning. I will explain that older adults can learn to harness their creativity at any age and that you can teach them to do this. I aim to equip you with information that you will need to develop a vigorous program of creativity-based cognitive training, using visual art-making as a means of mentally stimulating, creative self-expression.

Although visual art-making techniques and examples will be provided, the focus of the cognitive training work is on the process of art-making rather than the product produced. Older adults achieve cognitive benefits from the enjoyable, stimulating, and social process of art-making and art exhibiting; they are impeded by criticism on how art "should" look. In order to keep older adults focused on the process and inhibit feelings of anxiety and self-consciousness, it is very important to explain the cognitive, emotional, and social purposes behind creativity and art-making.

How to apply information presented within this text

Although the content within this book may be used with any person diagnosed with mild cognitive impairment (MCI), Alzheimer's disease (AD), or other dementia, it is best suited for older adults who are experiencing an onset of memory impairment but who are otherwise in good mental and physical health. Treatment for age-related cognitive declines is most effective at early stages (Alzheimer's Association 2010b).

This book does not claim that creativity can magically heal, or that it is a cure-all. I am not inventing a new method of creativity. I am simply explaining how artistic creativity is a natural means of cognitive training when structured according to therapeutic and cognitive training models. Many factors determine older adult late-life cognitive health, including genetic and medical factors. This book addresses the environmental, lifestyle and psychosocial factors only. For that reason, the content in this book works best in combination with other approaches such as through consultations with medical doctors, neurologists, and therapists (e.g. psychologists, art therapists, counselors).

Older adult mental/cognitive well-being can relate to one or several of five key areas: physical, social, emotional, spiritual, and mental. For instance, if an older adult is depressed because they are preoccupied with afterlife concerns, this depression may negatively impact their ability to function cognitively and therefore their memory (Butters *et al.* 2000). Table 1.1 demonstrates how each of the areas of older adult well-being relates to artistic creativity. However, one or more of these areas may need expert attention in order to ensure the wellness of the older adult.

Table 1.1 Domains and artistic creativity

Area of self-expression	Description
Physical self	Stress-management through art-making and the physical act of creating
Social self	Connection with others during creativity and community art exhibits
Emotional self	Self-exploration and insight of feelings during art-making
Spiritual self	Reflection on values and strengths throughout the creative process
Mental self	Development of knowledge and creative technical skill

To best apply the information within this text, you will need to create an atmosphere that promotes creative self-expression. This requires trust. The older adults must trust that they will be respected and that their contributions as valued members of their communities will be honored.

Memory is emotional; if you aim to improve memory and cognition, you must connect on an emotional level with the older adults. While anxiety and self-consciousness disempower and negatively affect older adults, authentic and personal connection does wonders for empowering them. Your sincere interest and engagement can transform their lives.

The adaptation of older adults to new circumstances is, in itself, a creative process which requires unconditional support and guidance. When older adults feel empowered, they are better able to take responsibility for their own lives, be flexible in interactions with others, and recognize their remaining strengths and abilities. A focus on self-expression encourages older adults to be proactive, to experience joy, and to focus their efforts on things that they can control.

Equipped with the information provided in this book, you will validate the aging experience, evolving identity, and self-worth of older adults. All of these factors promote positive brain states and opportunities for new neural connections within the brain (Diamond 2000). Through a focus on the unique self-expression needs of older adults, or gero-expressivity, you can do your part to help older adults live late-life to the fullest.

Overcoming ageism

Despite new understandings of the brain and research demonstrating that memory and cognitive abilities can be rehabilitated, negative views of aging are still widespread. In a recent publication, a manager of a facility serving older adults was quoted as saying, "It is hard to listen to older people. They are slow in speech and thought" (Allen *et al.* 1992, p.35 as cited in Neville 2008). Older people are subject to such prejudices as "being old doesn't matter" since it is akin to experiencing "a second childhood" (Allen *et al.* 1992, p.35 as cited in Neville 2008). Gerontologists have strongly argued that negative attitudes may be at the root of the worst problems that affect older people in US society today (Angus and Reeve 2006). The worst effect is that older adults themselves may begin to believe that they aren't valued by society and that debilitating memory loss is inevitable. This can make them feel hopeless, lonely, and defeated.

The brain responds to pain that results from physical harm in a similar way that it does to the pain that results from social rejection (Eisenberger and Lieberman 2004). For example, being considered an "out-group" member triggers a neural alarm that is similar to that of being physically assaulted. Many individuals experiencing social rejection go into a "fight, flight, or freeze" response. For older adults experiencing ageism, the response is more often "flight" or "freeze": they flee socially and become withdrawn, isolated, depressed, and anxious, and they may question their own self-worth.

Successful aging requires a positive self-image based on worth and value (Angus and Reeve 2006; Depp and Jeste 2009). By reading this book, you are part of the growing solution for what older adults fear most about aging: the loss of memory, respect, and, ultimately, a place in society. Working with older adults puts you in a unique position to help them overcome their fears and continue living life in meaningful ways. The successful older adult is passionate about getting the most out of life regardless of circumstances. You can help older adults to be significantly more successful and to be optimistic about maintaining cognitive abilities by using the strategies that I will be describing throughout this book.

By using the information in this book, you can help older adults to take an optimistic perspective. As you help them to creatively self-express, I encourage you to provide as much information as possible on the theory behind creative self-expression. Inform the older adults about why creative self-expression is not only fun and enjoyable but also a serious form of mental stimulation. In order to feel motivated, older adults need to understand why a pursuit matters. In this case, the reason for creativity is sustained and improved cognition.

As a creative professional, you have the opportunity to enhance older adult cognitive well-being. Yet the quality of the service that you or I or anyone provide(s) to older adults using this book can only be measured by the improvements demonstrated by the older adults themselves. Quality does not happen by chance: it occurs through a combination of focus, planning, strategy, warmth, and compassion. Table 1.2 summarizes the fundamental points discussed thus far and outlines the goals for consideration before reading on.

Table 1.2 Goals: memory training through creative self-expression

Goal	Purpose
1. Set and repeatedly state objectives	Reminds older adults that cognitive abilities can be trained
2. Set standards for older adult behavior	Keeps older adults focused
3. Measure older adult cognitive performance	Puts functioning into perspective; prevention and early intervention are most effective
4. Build and maintain relationships with and among older adults	Promotes feelings of safety, trust, and interconnectivity
5. Follow a structure that aligns with a cognitive training strategy	Creates predictable stimulation
6. Define the purpose of each creative activity	Focus on the aspect of the activity that provides the benefit: process over product
7. Organize opportunities for older adults to share and exhibit their artwork with each other and the community	Increases feelings of self-worth

Normal and abnormal aging

As individuals age, mental faculties change. The decline of some cognitive abilities, such as information-processing speed and word finding, is normal throughout the aging process (American Psychological Association 2010). The effects of normal aging do not impede daily living unless there is an onset of mild cognitive impairment (MCI) or another disorder (Rodgers *et al.* 2003).

In normal, healthy aging, the brain continuously changes its structure, producing new cells and fostering connections between them well into old age; this ability is referred to as neuroplasticity (Alzheimer's Association 2010b; Diamond 2000; Grady 2008). Neuroplasticity is what allows memory to be rehabilitated even in old age. The conductor of this process is the hippocampus, an area deep in the center of the brain. With stimulation, such as during memory training, the hippocampus' density and mass can increase and continue to effectively produce and develop brain cells (Stern 2009). Figure 1.1 illustrates the hippocampus and its location within the brain.

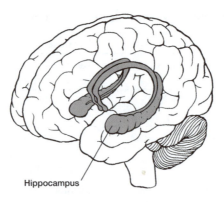

Hippocampus

Figure 1.1 Hippocampus in the brain

Alzheimer's disease

Alzheimer's disease (AD) is one of the most highly feared diseases; the only disease feared more is cancer (MetLife Foundation 2012). Yet many older adults do not understand the risk factors for Alzheimer's disease, nor do they understand what they can do to prevent or delay cognitive impairment. As a result, many older adults simply do nothing; they do not seek treatment for cognitive decline until the problem is severe. Severe impairment makes rehabilitation and improved cognitive performance highly unlikely. Preventative action is the most effective approach to older adult wellness. At early stages, cognitive impairment is reversible, but individuals with untreated cognitive impairment are almost three times more at risk for AD (Manly *et al.* 2008).

Mild cognitive impairment (MCI) is often marked by language disturbances (e.g. difficulty with sentence formation), attention deficits (e.g. difficulty following conversations), and deterioration of visuospatial skills (e.g. disorientation and an inability to appropriately use fine and/or gross motor skills) that interfere with daily functioning (Gauthier *et al.* 2006). MCI is associated with reduced blood flow through the brain's blood vessels and shrinkage of the hippocampus (Alzheimer's Association 2010a; Grady 2008). Plaques and tangles form among the branches of the brain cells' tree-like structures, which leads to an inability of cells to communicate with one another and eventual brain cell death (Alzheimer's Association 2010a). As neurons die, brain regions shrink, damaging areas involved in thinking, planning, and remembering (Alzheimer's Association

2010b; Chertkow, Verret and Bergmen 2001). This phenomenon is known as Alzheimer's disease and, due to the nature of cognitive decline, the line between Alzheimer's disease and MCI is often blurry.

Risk factors of memory loss

Factors affecting cognitive performance fall into two broad categories: genetic and lifestyle. Genetic factors are often addressed with medication or medical interventions. Lifestyle factors are a primary interest in this book as they can be addressed through a focus on increasing mental stimulation, decreasing stress, and improving socialization and mood.

Mental stimulation

Mental stimulation is an important factor in keeping the brain healthy and maintaining memory. In recent years, scientists have begun to draw a parallel between the brain and muscles: both need regular workouts to stay strong. Without consistent stimulation, the brain cannot remain plump and healthy, and the hippocampus shrivels, losing mass and density (Alzheimer's Association 2010a; Grady 2008).

When this happens, the hippocampus cannot generate new brain cells, new memories cannot be formed, and an older adult begins showing cognitive declines such as in language abilities and short-term memory (Czeh and Lucassen 2007; Diamond 2001). Active cognitive stimulation can keep the mass of the brain healthy and can be achieved through formal education, memory drills, or simply through a dynamic environment offering stimulating experiences (Perneczky *et al.* 2009; University of California 2007).

Motivation is an important factor in mental stimulation. Many mental exercises involve written language. However, not everyone wants to read, do crossword puzzles, or do memory drills to exercise their brain. Actually, not everyone can. An increasing number of older adults in the US don't speak English as a first language, and many older adults have grown up with limited access to formal education (Administration on Aging 2011). Older adult reading abilities might not be adequate for traditional cognitive training techniques such as reading and verbal drills (Elias and Wagster 2007; Sitzer *et al.* 2006). When using creative self-expression to target memory, an older adult's educational background and literacy level are no longer limiting factors.

Creative self-expression that offers mental stimulation can enrich an environment or older adult setting. The term "enriched environment" references a setting that can affect the brain's structure at any age and creates noticeable changes, such as in the hippocampus (Diamond 2001). An enriched environment promotes physical activity, socialization, and problem solving, leading to an increase in new neurons, or neurogenesis, and a substantial improvement in cognitive performance (Kempermann, Gast, and Gage 2002; Studenski *et al.* 2006).

Physical activity (e.g. manually creating art), problem solving (e.g. deciding on color), and socialization (e.g. describing artwork made) are all naturally incorporated into creative self-expression through the visual arts (Alders 2012). Through creative self-expression, an older adult can remain mentally stimulated in dynamic and fulfilling ways while receiving ongoing education as to new artistic techniques and processes.

Stress

Stress is another factor important to consider when maintaining brain fitness. In life, there is good stress, such as planning details of a wedding, and there is bad stress, such as watching a loved one battle cancer. Each type of stress sparks different emotions and impacts the brain differently.

Cortisol is the chemical that is released during stress and anxiety. In low levels, cortisol helps to create memories and link those memories to emotional life events. In low levels, stress can be healthy for the brain; however, long-term exposure to stress can have a neurotoxic effect on the brain and result in impaired memory (Caine and Caine 2006; Gauthier *et al.* 2006). Research indicates that high levels of stress can lead to a loss of neurons, particularly in the hippocampus region (Rothman and Mattson 2010).

Older adults may become more sensitive to stress as they age and experience stressors that are unique to aging, such as changes in lifestyle and financial status after retirement, death of relatives, loved ones, or close friends, and worries concerning dependence (Miller and O'Callaghan 2005; Rothman and Mattson 2010; Silver 1999). Additionally, many older adults feel anxious about "losing their marbles" regardless of whether they exhibit symptoms of memory decline (Miller and O'Callaghan 2005).

Older adults' beliefs about their memory are often emotionally charged and memory complaints are frequently linked to stress, anxiety, and depression (Butters *et al.* 2000; Tsai *et al.* 2008). Among older adults, worrying about memory is both an indication and a source of stress (Potter, Grealy, and O'Connor 2009). Actively worrying about memory increases cortisol concentrations in the brain, which can lead to loss of neurons; this can create a self-fulfilling prophecy wherein the worry of memory loss can also be the cause of that very memory loss (Gauthier *et al.* 2006).

Increasing older adults' confidence in themselves, their memory, and their abilities is very important for their well-being. Recent research on positive thinking and on mindfulness sheds light on the benefits of "here and now" exercises aimed to alleviate stress and worry. Having fun, experiencing joy, and being social all promote "here and now" experiences.

Depression and social isolation

Concealing emotions such as anxiety and depression in social settings (e.g. home environments with family) and pretending that nothing is wrong can be very stressful for an older adult and make him or her feel lonely and isolated, even in the company of others. This can trigger degraded memory, communication, and problem solving among older adults (Richards 2004). In contrast, emotional expressivity and an enhanced mood may protect against cognitive declines (Gray, Braver, and Raichle 2002). When asked to rate their health, older adults often use mood to determine whether or not they perceived themselves as healthy (Ostbye *et al.* 2006; Pruessner *et al.* 2004).

In late-life, aging individuals often bear witness to deaths of older adult friends and relatives. This increased likelihood of loss is itself a risk factor for depression (Greaves and Farbus 2006). Depression is one of the most common reasons older adults enter a long-term care facility; it affects up to 30 percent of people over the age of 65, and it severely impedes long-term cognitive health (Butters *et al.* 2000; Cole and Dendukuri 2003). Depression can lead to cognitive deficits in memory, attention, and motor skills (Gilley *et al.* 2004). The symptoms of depression resemble mild cognitive impairment, and because there are so many physiological similarities between depression and MCI, long-term depression is said to ultimately lead to MCI (Baune *et al.* 2006; Butters *et al.* 2000). When an older adult feels sad or depressed, they are less likely to want to socialize and interact, making a bad situation worse. Socialization is important for brain health as it engages diverse cognitive resources and distinct brain areas (Cummings 2003; Kempermann *et al.* 2002).

Improved mood is part of what makes creative self-expression effective for memory training. When provided opportunities for emotional gratification, an older adult can continue to find enjoyment through socializing and overcome feelings of loneliness. Bereavement and grief can be expressed in ways that bring self-confidence and feelings of self-worth. Older adults can create works of art expressing their feelings and also receive praise and encouragement for their creations. Self-worth leads to self-care, and never is this more important than in late-life. Artistic creativity, when used as a form of self-care among older adults, can provide a noticeable improvement in their lives.

Self-expression in late-life

Older adults will only use services to improve their memory if they desire to use those services. Older adults must enjoy the memory training exercises. Their opinion of the value and worth of intervention is what matters most because that is what will compel them to regularly attend the sessions. Creative sessions, when properly facilitated, can immensely add to their enjoyment of memory training. In recent studies, participants who engaged in creative self-expression during therapy reported more enjoyment, a higher likelihood to continue with therapy, and a desire to recommend therapy to family and friends (Pizarro 2004).

Providing opportunities for creative self-expression as memory training respects the older adult's lifetime of acquired wisdom and experience. Older adults have a lot to share and teach: they carry within them countless life stories. They need an audience with whom to share their wisdom. Creative professionals and other older adults, along with family and community members, can be that audience. Special attention and active listening when older adults are expressing themselves endows them with a sense of worth and importance.

Creativity means being original, and originality will only happen when older adults feel free and comfortable enough to express themselves without trying to meet others' expectations. When this process of self-discovery is met with positive feedback, the experience can be exciting and rewarding. During creative self-expression older adults make a conscious attempt to understand themselves while also learning how to present and relate themselves to others.

Creative self-expression can continuously help older adults to make sense of who they are as they age. This cultivates their drive to communicate their inner self to the world. This communication connects older adults to each other and to the greater community, keeping them active and emotionally secure.

Memory and cognitive health are dependent on emotional health. At all ages, but especially in late-life, emotional health relies upon an individual's ability to create a meaningful and socially valued personal identity. Identity and self-concept play a major role in behavior and can be a predictor of late-life depression and social withdrawal (Wilson and Ross 2003).

My experience and research with older adults has shown me that without a sense of self and a sense of worth, an older adult cannot and will not benefit from memory training. Creative professionals must prioritize the act of helping an older adult stay in touch with who they are and why that identity matters to the community. Selfhood is just as uncertain in old age as it is in other phases of life: "Who am I?" and "What good am I?" are questions that never go away. Self-expression is the way that identity is socially shared and is a direct means of helping an older adult find a meaningful and socially valued identity.

Art-making in groups has been shown to enhance socialization as well as to promote a more positive interpretation of "self" (Alders 2012; Reynolds and Prior 2006). The increase in socialization resulting from creative self-expression can be explained as follows: (a) art objects aid in communication and provide a point of reference during socializing (Abraham 2004; Malchiodi 2006; Østergaard 2008); (b) older adult art therapy participants can show friends and family their artwork, increasing discussions that may in turn (c) increase interest and motivation for continued socialization (Thoman, Sansone, and Pasupathi 2007).

Self-concept is continuously reshaped through autobiographical illustrations in art. Three overarching themes can be noted as recurrent throughout artwork in innumerable cultures and across diverse time periods: a sense of self, a sense of place, and a sense of community (Anderson and Milbrandt 2005). All three are relevant to identity, and self-expression through art-making reaffirms healthy identity.

When an older adult has a firm sense of their worth and value, their interactions with others promote social solidarity. Atmospheres of social solidarity promote brain health and create an enriched and stimulating environment that naturally enhances cognitive functioning. When the brain is under stress due to fear or sadness, for example, it cannot think clearly, let alone remember vividly. Joy, trust, and comfort prepare the brain to create new neural connections and produce new cells.

Concerns, fears, and insecurities about what others may think can result in a censorship of self-expression. Emotions can be communicated through non-verbal channels, one of which is art-making. Compared to candid verbal descriptions of feelings, visual self-expression often feels safer. It can also be rich with symbolism and personal meaning, making it a suitable means of self-expression for those who have difficulty finding the words to describe their emotions.

Creative self-expression through art-making allows older adults to develop visual representations of who they are, what they feel and think, and who they want to be. They can take beliefs and feelings associated with memories and turn those experiences into something tangible. Artwork can be a concrete way to share inner experiences, which creates the potential for older adults to feel understood by others.

The events that happen in an older adult's life can become a source of inspiration for creativity. Every experience, be it festive, saddening, or transitional, can be fuel for artwork. Allowing experiences to have a productive purpose provides older adults opportunities for reflection and growth. They may find inner strength that they never knew existed. An artwork expressing loss can also provide an older adult with admiration and respect.

Encouraging mental stimulation through expressive art-making

When using art-making to address self-expression, socialization, and mental stimulation, knowing and understanding what is meant by the word "art" is important. Art is a term for which there are many different definitions, but for this book, I will use this one: the conscious use of visual materials to portray aspects of personal experiences, emotions, and identity in order to engage creative imagination. The word "art" will not be used to describe the creation of an object for decorative or utilitarian purposes. The benefits of art-making are in the expressive components, not in marks themselves (De Petrillo and Winner 2005). Therefore, the definition of art will relate to a representation of reality—even if that reality is so personal, emotional, and abstract that only the older adult who created it understands it.

In art, a symbolic message, or meaning, that is created provides an aesthetic experience or a state of sensuous cognition (Berleant 1964). A crucial element of an aesthetic experience is having a neural response similar to re-experiencing a personal memory (Freedberg and Gallese 2007). This neural response could happen when viewing or making artwork. While viewing a work of art, an older adult may be vividly reminded of a life experience. When creating artwork, an older adult may work towards portraying a moment in his or her life as it was experienced; this becomes a "selective re-creation of reality" (Rand 1969, p.45).

Art is a translation of an experience and can arouse a mixture of two types of memories: voluntary memories, which can be recalled at will, and the more vivid involuntary memories, which are directly related to sensory experiences and only able to be triggered by a sensory cue (Epstein 2002). Voluntary memories leave out details (such as color, scent, and temperature, along with the "feeling" of the moment) in favor of factual accuracy and a general knowledge of the experience (Epstein 2002, p.7). Art evokes a network of associations that conveys the "essence" of an experience and can cause involuntary memories to come to the surface, allowing the older adult to re-experience the sensory details of the past (Epstein 2002).

Incorporating creativity into older adult identity through art-making

Creative behavior is said to epitomize adaptability, an essential skill for today's older adults (Fisher 1999). When older adults create art, they are no longer "elderly," "senior," or "aged"; they are "artists," "creative," and "expressive." With this comes the opportunity for a positive and life-affirming transformation in identity.

My research has demonstrated that diverse older adults may quickly come to understand the association between art-making and wellness (Alders 2012). Much of the documented folk healing among Asian, African-American, and Latino cultures incorporates the creation and use of art, such as in the form of images and pictorial symbolism (Graham *et al.* 2005). That said, older adults may be wary about trying new things. Some may fear failure or question the purpose behind the creativity. Creativity through art-making can be taught in a manner that promotes cognitive stimulation while decreasing anxiety about "making it look right." A highly structured, predetermined, and sequential format can provide a sense of comfort for older adults when learning something new.

In 1945, the US was recovering from the Great Depression, and there was an inequality of wealth and income. Most people worked overtime and gave up their leisure activities and even schooling to make money or to fight in the war. Creativity was largely viewed as a leisure activity by this population and therefore was not prioritized (Fisher 1999). For many older adults, this may be the first time in their lives that they have allowed themselves to be creative for the sake of being creative.

Older adults who are encouraged to "draw how you feel" without explicit instruction on how to do so may look at a blank page and experience anxiety rather than a feeling of relief or creative inspiration. This may be especially true if the older adult has no previous experience working with art materials. Learners experiencing anxiety, boredom, and frustration are likely to be stifled. An initial approach of "Go for it!" can be ineffective and even counterproductive when an older adult lacks technical skill or self-confidence.

Providing information in an increasing order of complexity will help motivate older adults toward creative self-expression. After they are introduced to basic concepts and technical skills, they can be provided with the opportunity for a self-directed approach that is meaningful to them and conducive to their particular emotional and expressive needs. To help an older adult engage creatively, you might sequence session content to target behavior first, thought second, and then emotion-centered self-expression last.

Creative behavior

Simply put, creativity is a process of making something. At this basic level, creative behavior is a kinesthetic process that creates a feedback loop. Older adults can paint marks on a page and receive positive feedback from those around them. This can, in turn, motivate an older adult to continue being creative in increasingly complex ways. To begin, creativity simply requires overt action so that the behavior can be reinforced and compelled to continue (Cunia 2005). Table 1.3 outlines the steps that can be implemented to assist older adults in creative behavior (Cunia 2005; Ertmer and Newby 1993).

Table 1.3 Steps to elicit creative behavior

Technique	Description
Guided steps	Reinforcing behavior that is progressively more creative whether or not that behavior is considered a success by the older adult
Reinforcement	Providing praise/recognition to the older adult for creative behavior
Modeling	Demonstrating the behavior desired from the older adult
Cueing	Reminding the older adult about the timing needed for a behavior
Pattern recognition	Helping the older adult identify differences in circumstance to decide on appropriate creative behavior

1. GUIDED STEPS

No one can be expected to immediately be creative if they have never before been involved in creative pursuits. Providing older adults with verbal and social rewards for little-by-little achievements will benefit their confidence and their skill set (Cunia 2005; Eisenberger and Shanock 2003; Huitt 1994). You can accomplish this by starting off with small, manageable creative directives and then progressively moving towards more complex tasks (Ormrod 1999). For example, rather than saying, "Paint a scene using the materials in front of you," you might focus on demonstrating how the texture of a paint brush feels (e.g. mop brush, fan brush) and then direct an older adult to put water on a brush, dip it in paint, and then drag it across the page. You can direct the older adults' attention to the type of lines created by the brush. This sequential approach is much less intimidating.

You may notice that if you host creative self-expression groups in a community setting, some older adults will come and just watch. They may even refuse to participate. These older adults may be interested in art-making but reluctant to get involved. Saying, "We're glad you came back today!" will reinforce their presence among the group members and increase their level of comfort as compared to saying, "C'mon! Sit down! You know you want to!" Commending their passive role is far more beneficial than urging them to join. Eventually, they may join, but allowing them to do so on their own terms is important.

2. REINFORCEMENT

Older adults may worry that they are doing things "the wrong way" when trying to be creative. Rewarding them with immediate praise after each progressive attempt will help them to gain confidence and continue being creative (Huitt 1994; Nevin and Grace 2000; Thomas 1988). A teacher may praise the work while assisting in an external focus: "Good job. Notice the parallel hatching lines that were created by the fan brush. That is what you wanted. Well done."

3. MODELING

Older adults, like most people, learn by example. Allowing older adults to observe a technique as it is performed will benefit their overall learning (Bransford, Brown, and Cocking 2000; Huitt 1994). For example, during a workshop with a guest artist, you might say, "Watch how she shapes veins on the leaves with the fan brush." Modeling key aspects of creativity until the older adults are able to work without assistance will be important for their success; you will be responsible for passing on knowledge of the creative process rather than simply instructing content. Patience is very valuable, as older adults will require repetition.

4. Cueing

Creativity is often all about timing. Older adults may need assistance in remembering to act at a specific time. A cue should be provided just before the action is expected rather than after it is performed incorrectly (Huitt 1994). For instance, you may find yourself saying something like, "Once you place the brush down, remember to quickly lift it. Ready? Ok. Press…hooold it…now…lift it quickly… Good. The timing was just right on that one."

5. Pattern recognition

Creativity requires sensitivity to timing and situation. What is effective in one set of circumstances may not be effective in another set of circumstances (Delahaye and Ehrich 2008; Huitt 1994). You can assist older adults in learning to differentiate circumstances: "You've decided to paint a water scene and water techniques require a different process and a different brush. We won't be using a fan brush today. Remember that soaking the page with water, using a mop brush will make a water scene… Yes, that is a mop brush; you picked the right one. Wonderful."

Creative thought

Once an older adult becomes more comfortable with creative behavior and learns a foundation of technical skill, they can begin developing a "cognitive architecture" related to creative thought and beliefs (Carruthers 2007). At this stage, an older adult can begin to apply cognitive strategies and problem-solving tactics (Huitt 2003; Ormrod 1999). For instance, an older adult would evaluate what they are seeing on the page (e.g. color, line) and then ask themselves, "Was this my goal? Is this how I wanted it to look?" This perceptive sensory information is then processed in short-term memory: "What was it that I learned about creating hatching lines with a fan brush? How did hatching look again (i.e. requires visualizing)?" As an older adult continues to do this, the information becomes transferred to long-term memory, and creativity ultimately becomes the reorganization of information (Huitt 2003). Sorting and encoding information into short-term memory and long-term memory enables many different combinations of thoughts and memories; this results in heightened mental stimulation (Bracey and Dorn 2001).

Creative thinking requires confidence and incentive, both of which can be gained with the steps outlined in Table 1.4.

Table 1.4 Steps for encouraging confident creative thinking

Focus of session	Description
Joy	Encouraging an older adult to focus on the process of creating
Effort and persistence	Setting goals that are easily obtainable
Achievement	Provide opportunities for social acknowledgement of achievements
Standards and goals	Informing older adults of goals in advance so behavior can be directed
Observation	Focusing on creative growth visible in the artwork
Evaluation	Promoting a futuristic attitude and using current learning as an opportunity for future achievement
Reaction	Expressing positive responses to experiences rather than accomplishments

1. Joy

Like most people, older adults will continue to do what they find enjoyable. Although there is a lot to appreciate about being creative, each person will enjoy a different aspect of the process. Allowing older adults to explore their own preferences is important. For example, you may encourage the older adults to use whatever colors attract them, whether or not these colors relate to real life.

2. Effort and persistence

Older adults will put more effort into pursuits that they consider possible to achieve (Delahaye and Ehrich 2008). While working with older adults, you can increase motivation and persistence by setting goals that are obtainable and breaking down complex tasks into smaller steps. For instance, if an older adult wants to paint a picture of their grandchild but has no artistic ability or training, you, as a creative professional, may break down this process into manageable steps. Rather than say "Paint the portrait on canvas," you may instead instruct the following steps over the course of several weeks:

- Bring in an enlarged, photo-copied picture of the grandchild.

- Using a ruler, draw lines vertically and horizontally, creating a grid on the image.

- Draw those same lines over a stretched canvas, creating a larger grid.

- Copy the shapes within each grid from the photo onto the larger grid on the canvas.

- Paint the "cool colors."

- Paint the "warm colors."

- Paint the skin tones.

- Paint the highlights with whites and yellows.

- Paint the outer edges of the stretched canvas black.

- Sign the work in the lower right corner.

Steps, such as the above, take a daunting task and make it a sequential process that can be achieved. This concept leads to the third area to be considered.

3. ACHIEVEMENT

Accomplishments and achievements increase feelings of self-efficacy and confidence, which may result in higher interest in creativity. You can provide older adults with a sense of achievement by simply praising the effort behind their work ("Wow. You really captured the feeling-of-the-moment in your art piece. Looking at the piece, I feel calm and tranquil") or by putting on an art show and inviting their families ("The art show was such a success. All of your creativity was really admired! I'm sure you noticed all of the attention that your work received").

4. STANDARDS AND GOALS

When older adults know what is expected of them, they can be free to focus on how to achieve those goals rather than wondering, "What do I do? What next?" To help an older adult to focus, you could inform them of the goal in advance: "Today, we are going to create three quick drawings on the theme of family. The goal of doing this is to focus on getting multiple thoughts on paper as fast as possible. Draw each as quickly as you can. Use a material that you feel most comfortable using. Don't worry about drawing details. You will have three minutes to draw each drawing. Sketch lightly and quickly."

5. OBSERVATION

Whether or not an older adult accomplishes a goal in its entirety, they are always working towards improvement. If the goal was to draw three drawings, and they accomplished one, that's OK; but they should still make a mental note of how many they accomplished to focus on increasing that number with time. You might facilitate this by saying, "OK. Time's up. How many quick sketches did you do? However many you did, you worked hard! Reward yourself. Stand up. Stretch. Walk around and view the work of others and your own." Your consistent positivity and support is crucial for older adult success.

6. EVALUATION

Although the products created during art-making have their benefits, the focus should remain on the process. Throughout the process of art-making, older adults engage in self-exploration and use effortful attention to control their thoughts and behavior. This is mental and emotional exercise. When evaluating their artwork, older adults should be encouraged to have a forward-thinking attitude and to use current learning as an opportunity for future achievement: "Every time you create, you have the opportunity to learn something about yourself and the world. What did you learn today that will help you tomorrow?"

7. REACTION

Positive emotions can be very healthy for older adults while stress and anxiety may be counterproductive to targeting memory skills. If an older adult experiences stress and anxiety in reaction to the creative process, they may be progressing through the creative stages too quickly and may be best directed back to the previous level (i.e. creative behavior).

Older adults who have a positive response to their creative experiences are more likely to continue being creative. Be sure to acknowledge their achievements and reaffirm the goal: "Having completed this project, you should all be very proud of yourselves. You worked hard to express yourself! Congratulations! That's what being an artist is about. It's not about how the art looks. It's about how making the art made you feel."

Creative self-expression

Once older adults have gotten used to behaving in creative ways and using creative problem-solving with a degree of confidence, they can begin to integrate creativity into self-expression. At this stage, they will begin to focus their energy on their own emotional state, using these feelings to guide creativity.

In previous stages, creativity was evaluated based on specific observable objectives; at this stage, the evaluation of creativity is much more subjective. Now, creativity becomes centered on the construction of meaning based on life experiences, and at this cognitive and symbolic level, creativity results from exploration (Schweitzer and Stephenson 2008).

Creative self-expression is the highest level of creativity and is a very personal process. Creativity is the result of encouraged discoveries intersecting with self-directed behavior as well as transformational and reflective thinking. During creative self-expression, the emphasis is on cooperative exploration rather than individual exploration (Schweitzer and Stephenson 2008).

At this level, a deep understanding of older adults' internal worlds is necessary to engage the older adults. Any structure provided to older adults should give them a degree of autonomy and allow them to choose among several activities based on personal motivations. This allows reflective exploration to take place. In Chapter 5 of this book, you will find protocols that allow for the incorporation of memories, beliefs, and values into the process while providing creative freedom. For example, the following directive grants a choice in materials, techniques, and partners because none of these aspects are specified: "Aging allows for life transformations to occur. Create an image showing how you are transforming. Get into groups and discuss the work that you created." Table 1.5 outlines concepts to assist older adults in creativity at this level.

Table 1.5 Concepts related to creative self-expression

Concepts	Description
Self-reflection	Introspection during creativity that leads to insight regarding identity
Personal interpretations	Explaining and describing artwork based on a distinctive viewpoint
Meaning and symbolism	Representing experiences, thoughts, feelings, and memories in artwork
Negotiated perspectives	Adapting viewpoints based on shared perspectives in a creative setting
Everyday experiences	Incorporating sensory knowledge from daily life into art depictions

1. SELF-REFLECTION

Older adults have a lifetime of experience which can provide a source of inspiration during art-making. Reflection during the creative process can be a source of self-knowledge as well as a fount for creative ideas. Self-reflection can be incited with simple exercises such as: "Close your eyes and remember a time that relates to the object that you are holding in your hand. Visualize that memory. What colors are present? What textures?"

2. PERSONAL INTERPRETATIONS

Older adults have developed unique viewpoints, preferences, and feelings. When two older adults view the same work of art, each person may "see" something different. Personal interpretations are valuable because they reveal insights about the viewers; their interpretations are often projections of their own experiences and may even relate to the older adult's culture and ethnicity.

To encourage personal interpretations, you may show older adults a piece of art and guide them through the process of personal interpretation by asking thoughtful questions such as (Anderson and Milbrandt 2005): "Describe what you see in this image. What is happening? Does this artwork represent a universal human need? If so, what need? If you could name this piece, what would you name it?" The memories recalled while viewing the work could then form the basis for their own artwork, using the following prompt: "Recreate the memory you had using the medium of your choice."

3. MEANING AND SYMBOLISM

Creativity is an action-oriented process that cultivates meaning and symbolism (Lusebrink 2010). Objects and depictions may assume a different significance than their face value. A painted apple may represent temptation for one older adult, but to another that same apple may represent summer afternoons on a farm with family. When working with older adults, explore the significance of what is depicted in their artwork: "I see that you included flowers in your image. What memories do flowers bring up for you? How did you feel and what did you think about while painting the flowers? How do you feel now, viewing the representation that you created? What does this painting reveal about you? What mood does the painting take on? Do you recall thinking differently about flowers when you were younger?"

4. NEGOTIATED PERSPECTIVES

Being creative in a group setting offers older adults the opportunity to think about things from a different perspective. For one person, a painting may be saddening; for another it may exude a liberating feeling. The negotiation of different perspectives fosters mental stimulation and creative growth. You may encourage this kind of negotiation by having group members provide responses to the art of another group member: "Thank you for sharing your artwork. Members of the group may be reminded of their own experiences based on your drawing. Let's hear some of what your art brings to mind for them and hear their stories. Who would like to share the thoughts and feelings that come up when looking at this work?"

5. EVERYDAY EXPERIENCES

Daily life is full of sensory experiences, and an artwork that portrays life can transmit potent feelings and thoughts. Art can portray the feeling of a moment and, because of personal interpretation, it can seem just as real. It can bridge together multiple lives: a grandmother can paint depictions of her grandchildren while she lives alone in a community center. Additionally, art can reposition older adults as a center of attention which affirms their worth and value to the community. To facilitate this, you might organize an art show that exhibits the work of older adults and allows them to share their memories with their families.

Summary

As you guide older adults towards creative self-expression, remember that the goal of the sessions is to engage, stimulate, and involve older adults socially in a way that makes them feel comfortable. Tailoring techniques and organizing the environment to meet their needs is the best way to foster collaboration between you and the older adult and to ensure their happiness, which is the most important part of the process. Continually reminding an older adult about the purpose of self-expression will keep them focused on the process of being creative, through which they can explore their relationships, identity, and interests through art-making and be motivated toward meaningful social interaction.

Regardless of the level of creativity that is comfortable for the older adult, be it creative behavior, thought or self-expression, older adults will benefit from the opportunity to see themselves in a new light (e.g. as artists), share and discuss images in a group, and feel like valuable members of a community. All of this offers positive stimulation and can contribute to neurological wellness. The following chapter focuses on the importance of putting older adult feelings first and foremost.

Chapter 2

HAPPINESS, SOCIAL CREATIVITY, AND THE BRAIN

KEY CONCEPT: Emotions affect memory
and the aging experience.

WORDBANK
(Definitions can be found throughout the chapter.)

1	EEGs	9	Reminiscence
2	Neurotransmitters	10	Visual elements
3	Dopamine	11	Symbiotic
4	Serotonin	12	Mandala
5	Acetylcholine	13	Value
6	Gamma	14	Saturation
7	Alpha	15	Stratification
8	Beta	16	Rorschach

Guiding older adults towards creative self-expression often requires a special sensitivity to their feelings and mood. In order to be socially engaged and stimulated, older adults must feel good about being involved in the session. Their happiness within the session can make or break their motivation to explore group relationships, their identity, and their interests in art-making. For this reason, it is essential to tailor the sessions to optimize opportunities to enhance mood. In order to do this, a creative professional must understand happiness on a multifaceted level while also understanding how art-making can potentially affect mood and feelings in a social setting.

Happiness and creative self-expression

Happiness is essential at any age, but especially in later life. Happiness involves feelings such as pleasure and comfort, and can range from contentment to extreme joy. Emotions and thoughts affect how the body functions, and there is extensive evidence of the connection between physical and mental well-being. Older adults in particular may be more aware of this connection, as they often equate mood with physical and mental health (Ostbye *et al.* 2006).

Positive mood has three primary effects on cognition among older adults: it increases focus, attention, and decision-making (Charles, Mather, and Carstensen 2003). If an older adult is happy, he or she is better able to pay attention and to perform memory tasks, such as recalling a person's name or using past information to make an informed decision (Van Gerven 2002). Positive experiences and an elevated mood help an older adult's brain to function optimally.

The hippocampus, an area of the brain that is critical to an individual's ability to remember ongoing life experiences, is among the first areas affected by cognitive impairment and Alzheimer's disease. It resides in the limbic system (i.e. the emotion center) of the brain, and it exchanges synaptic transmissions with the prefrontal cortex (i.e. the center for planning, complex cognition, decision-making, and social behavior; Davidson 2003; Stern 2009). In other words, the hippocampus creates an overlap between emotional and cognitive functioning. Therefore, emotion-centered activities like art-making may provide a means of "working around" and even rehabilitating cognitive deficits (Stern 2009).

Many researchers firmly hold that cognitive interventions like memory training do not and will not work for older adults who are experiencing emotional distress, such as depression (Mateer, Sira, and O'Connell 2005). For this reason, emotion-focused techniques, like those incorporated during creative self-expression, may be more effective than cognition-focused techniques alone. Emotion-focused techniques incorporate therapeutic conversations about feelings and can target improved mood, thereby potentially alleviating emotional distress (Mateer *et al.* 2005; Chertkow *et al.* 2001). When older adults are guided through a creative process, they can relax and take initiative for their own enjoyment. This state of relaxed enjoyment during creativity can improve memory training outcomes (Alders 2012).

Elevating mood during creative sessions

Elevating mood among older adults is a strengths-based approach. Late-life brings an abundance of social and emotional knowledge, and studies have repeatedly shown that emotion regulation improves with advancing age (Williams *et al.* 2006). As people age, they become more interested in eliminating negativity and are better able to solve emotionally salient problems when compared with younger adults; as a result, older adults frequently report being happier than younger adults (Blanchard-Fields 2007; Scheibe and Blanchard-Fields 2009).

Happiness and self-expression are interrelated and can create a feedback loop, meaning that creative self-expression can spark experiences of pleasure and improved mood, while improved mood may increase the likelihood that a person will creatively self-express (Pannells and Claxton 2008). While a positive mood can help an older adult to be creative, being creative can help an older adult to have a positive mood.

In terms of improving memory, creative self-expression and positive mood have a symbiotic relationship, and work together to promote brain health. A positive mood allows the older brain to take in a higher level of rich sensory information (e.g. smell, sounds, colors) and facilitates a broader repertoire of thoughts and feelings, making additional cognitive material available for processing (Charles *et al.* 2003). The optimistic brain is more alert to its surroundings, and this fuels creative inspiration, and creative inspiration, in turn, can spark feelings of pleasure (De Petrillo and Winner 2005).

The combination of positive mood (e.g. joy) and positive activities (e.g. artistic creativity) align with concepts presented on positive psychology by Martin Seligman in his 2002 book, *Authentic Happiness*. Seligman describes three categories of positive emotions that are brought on by external stimuli and align with creative self-expression: bodily pleasures, higher pleasures, and gratification. Table 2.1 outlines how creative self-expression sessions can provide opportunities for each of these "pleasures of the moment."

Table 2.1 Categories of positive emotion and creative experience

Category	Creative Experience
Bodily pleasures	Enjoying a tactile sensation (e.g. squishing paint between paper)
Higher pleasures	Having an aesthetic experience while viewing a work of art
Gratifications	Being absorbed in the process of creating something meaningful

BODILY/SENSORY PLEASURES

Creative behavior, or the simple process of making something, can provide a sense of pleasure. The physical act of creating is directly related to the senses (e.g. touch, sight) and does not necessarily require extensive thought, planning, or skill. For instance, an older adult may be directed to create Rorschach blots by squirting a combination of colors on one side of a page and then folding the page in two. This creates an effect in which an abstract pattern is duplicated on both sides of the page (see Figure 2.1). The older adult may be excited by the forms and appealing color patterns that emerge. The older adult might physically enjoy feeling the cool paint squish between their hands as they fold the paper in half.

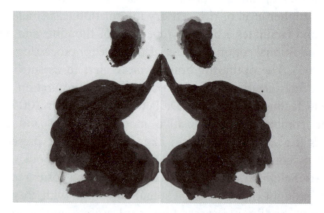

Figure 2.1 Rorschach blot done with paint on folded paper

Body pleasures, such as those evoked during creative behavior, are rooted in the here-and-now experience. These pleasures allow the older adult to experience their body's physical sensations to the fullest and, as a result, to feel "alive." Bodily pleasures throughout the art-making process are fleeting, but they can quickly enhance mood and heighten the older adults' awareness of their surroundings as they prepare themselves for additional bodily pleasures. Art therapy research has shown that such sensory exploration allows older adults with cognitive impairment to become emotionally expressive and thereby bypass cognitive deficits and, in some cases, rehabilitate functioning (Alders 2012).

HIGHER ORDER PLEASURES

In contrast to bodily pleasures, which are rooted in the kinesthetic act of making something, higher pleasures come from internal thoughts and cognitive efforts, such as when an older adult begins to apply problem-solving tactics to his or her artwork. For instance, an older adult may view the image that resulted from the Rorschach activity and begin to brainstorm the aesthetics, observing and evaluating the forms and shapes: What does this look like? What does this remind me of? An image like Figure 2.1 may evoke associations like two people praying, a surprised face, or two people playing patty cake.

While bodily pleasures relate to the here and now, higher pleasures are associated with past, present, and future perceptual and affective experiences (Seligman 2002). For instance, an older adult may be reminded of when her grandchildren used to play patty cake, or she may express the intention to teach them a patty cake game that she once played as a child. In either case, higher pleasures can result in a "cognitive architecture" that is produced by pleasing thoughts, which in turn stimulate additional thoughts that may be pleasing (Carruthers 2007).

Through such a process of thoughtfulness, higher pleasures may also promote a state of reminiscence. Reminiscence is a process wherein older adults draw on memory while sharing stories about their life and their past (Butler 1980; Woolhiser-Stallings 2010). Research has demonstrated that older adults experience significant cognitive improvement following guided reminiscence. In addition to being a beneficial part of regimented therapy, older adults may naturally practice reminiscence during social and creative activities such as art-making.

The activity occurring within the brain comes in the form of distinct, measurable, and electro-chemical brain waves. Differing brain waves are distinguished by factors such as speed, voltage, and rhythm (Braverman 2005). These factors create differences in the appearances of each type of brain wave when graphed using an EEG.

To understand the nature of brain waves, consider the ocean (see Figure 2.4). Waves can appear as tiny ripples on the surface of the water or as giant undulations of water swallowing up the ocean itself. In nature, many factors affect the type of aquatic waves that come in from the ocean onto the beach, and each type of wave affects the beach differently. Some waves may build the beach up by depositing small shells while other waves can strip the beach of sand and plant-life. Likewise, some electro-chemical states can build up positive feelings, while other states can leave older adults feeling depleted.

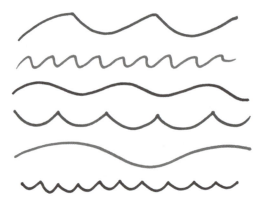

Figure 2.4 Comparison between ocean waves and brain waves

Brain waves represent the release of chemicals known as neuro-transmitters that affect the brain in diverse ways. Neurotransmitters are brain chemicals that send information to cells, organs, and glands (Chudler 2013). There is a relationship between a released neurotransmitter and the corresponding brain wave type; as a result, brain waves represent variations in communication between neurons (Braverman 2005; Chudler 2013).

Think of a brain wave as the sound of a voice, and the neurotransmitter as the message being conveyed. A voice could whisper "Be happy" or it could shout it quickly and enthusiastically: "BE HAPPY!" In either case, the volume and tone are intrinsically linked to the overall impact of the message. What and how something is communicated matters in both verbal and neural exchange (Braverman 2005). Similarly, brain waves and neurotransmitters reflect and affect the functioning of the brain in terms of thoughts, moods, and actions (Chudler 2013). For instance, if that same referenced voice representing brain waves were to be distorted by irregular speed and rhythm—"BeEe HhhapPpy"—the result may resemble cognitive impairment in that the message would not be readily understood (Braverman 2005).

Neurotransmitters and creativity

Life experiences can affect neurotransmitters and brain waves. However, neurotransmitters and brain waves can also affect the perception of life experiences. If someone is happy, they may notice positive things happening around them; if someone notices something positive happening around them, they may feel happy. Because of this, external stimuli (e.g. life experiences) and internal stimuli (e.g. brain waves and neurotransmitters) can be equally powerful and can influence mood and health among older adults independent of one another. Although a creative professional may not be able to affect an older adult's external life experiences (e.g. with whom they live, loss of loved ones), a creative professional may be able to affect an older adult's internal stimuli in a way that promotes a positive outlook and the perception of positive life experiences. To accomplish this, creative professionals will benefit from seeing the brain as an adaptable and ever-changing ecosystem.

Understanding brain waves that result from art-making may help a professional to positively affect an older adult's internal stimuli. Creative professionals can provide art-making directives that can either "calm the sea" or create "ripples in the water," depending on what would most likely enhance the older adult's mood. The three neurotransmitters (and corresponding brain waves) that relate to both happiness and creativity—and therefore pertain to creativity-based memory training—are acetylcholine (gamma), dopamine (beta), and serotonin (alpha). Table 2.2 illustrates this relationship.

Table 2.2 Neurotransmitters, brain waves, and memory training

Brain wave	Experience	Effect	Neurotransmitter
Gamma	Enhanced memory, speed of thought, improved learning, intellectual functioning	Assists memory, provides inspiration	Acetylcholine
Beta	Energy, excitement, focus, attention, activities and interaction, concentration	Increases cerebral blood flow, creates motivation	Dopamine
Alpha	State of balance, meditation, enjoyment, pleasure	Calms the mind and body, aids visualization	Serotonin

Serotonin

The bodily pleasures that arise during creative behaviors can evoke enjoyment and calm the mind and body. When this occurs, alpha brain states prompt the releases of serotonin. Serotonin is known as the "happy hormone." Serotonin is a chemical that calms anxiety, relieves depression, and helps older adults maintain a positive mood.

Serotonin is linked to basic motor activity and therefore intrinsic to creative behavior. Serotonin neurons may be released in response to repetitive behaviors like gluing collage photos onto paper, cutting out shapes, or using broad strokes to paint a single color onto a large canvas. The physical, rhythmic, and repetitive acts performed during art-making can increase serotonin activity.

Furthermore, serotonin assists an older adult in creating bodily pleasures by facilitating a here-and-now experience. Serotonin facilitates excellent hand–eye coordination and mental flexibility. The mind–body connection is heightened by serotonin release. Creative directives that may trigger serotonin release are outlined in Table 2.3.

Table 2.3 Serotonin and creativity

Serotonin Factor	Creative Directive Promoting Factor
Hand–eye coordination	Repetitively adding strokes of color within a confined area
Bodily pleasure	Focusing on the sensation of the materials
Mind–body connection	Breathing deeply and moving slowly and methodically
Self-esteem	Feeling of renewed identity through the creative process; choosing colors without self-judgment and based on impulse and intuition

To promote the release of serotonin through alpha brain waves among older adults, a creative professional may provide a mandala directive to an older adult. A mandala is a geometrical image which is symbolic of wholeness, and completeness, and this activity is said to be soothing and relaxing while requiring repetitive movement. During a mandala directive, an older adult may repetitively select colors and create repeating or mirrored patterns within a contained circular shape (see Figure 2.5). Intuition and spontaneity may guide the decision process and therefore fall in line with alpha brain states. Additionally, an older adult may visualize how the end product may look, which is aided by alpha brain states (Vanlierde and Wanet-Defalque 2005).

Figure 2.5 Mandala

Through alpha brain waves and the release of serotonin during creative behavior, older adults may experience feelings of pleasure, happiness, self-esteem, serenity, relaxation, and a sense of well-being. This state prepares the brain to engage in cognitive training. The hippocampus, the area responsible for the formation of new brain cells, is affected by serotonin levels. Depletion in serotonin decreases the brain's ability to engage in neurogenesis, or the development of new neurons and neural connections within the brain. Serotonin is an important factor involved in the hippocampus' ability to promote memory. When brain rhythms are at alpha, this creates an optimal neural environment for the creation of new brain cells (Berumen *et al.* 2012).

Dopamine

Higher pleasures such as positive thoughts and ideas that arise during creative activity are associated with beta brain waves. Beta brain waves correspond with the release of dopamine and can increase an older adult's mental alertness. During a state of higher pleasure, dopamine motivates older adults to explore ways to apply cognitive strategies and problem-solving tactics to their artworks. Through dopamine, older adults are more aware of their surroundings and can take in more sensory information (e.g. color, shape, texture).

Dopamine is known to enhance an older adult's energy level, excitement, motivation, and achievement orientation. Conversely, dopamine can impede a person's ability to verbally communicate their feelings; artistic creativity provides an alternate means of communicating those feelings. To promote an increase in the production of dopamine through beta brain states and provide a means for expressing feelings, a creative professional may direct an older adult to think through color selection when creating a mandala. The professional may present the older adult with a list of emotion words and then instruct the older adult to pick three emotion words that describe how they are currently feeling. The older adult would then be instructed to associate those emotion words to colors, and to use the associated colors to create the mandala design inside of a contained circular shape. Those colors would be chosen to represent feelings but also to accomplish a concrete goal. Table 2.4 outlines creative directives that may promote dopamine release.

Table 2.4 Dopamine and creativity

Dopamine factor	Creative directive promoting factor
Divergent thinking/brain storming	Brainstorm words that associate with feelings
Abstract thought	Associate colors to those feelings
Setting goals	Complete a mandala using those colors
Long-term planning	Decide where to hang the completed mandala in the home
Adrenaline production	Feel excited for others to see the mandala

While serotonin facilitates a relaxing experience of creativity, dopamine facilitates a more active experience that aids in a sense of accomplishment. Creative professionals can promote dopamine production during artistic creativity by focusing on motivators such as achievement, recognition, and improved abilities. Older adults' artwork can be shared and discussed in a group setting and then put on display once it is completed to promote feelings of achievement and recognition.

Dopamine, like serotonin, assists the functioning of the hippocampus; while serotonin promotes neurogenesis, dopamine promotes neuroplasticity. Dopamine helps the hippocampus determine which information should be encoded into memory and therefore determines which synaptic connections between neurons should be strengthened and which should be weakened. This allows changes in the overall structure and pattern of clustered/connected neurons within the brain. Neurons that are not connected to other neurons eventually die, so dopamine's role in promoting or dissolving synaptic connections is crucial (Berumen et al. 2012).

In addition to promoting neuroplasticity, dopamine plays an important role in maintaining older adult status within the community. In many societies, older adults are thought to be wise, and to give worthwhile advice to younger generations. Whether or not this is universally true, dopamine production makes both wisdom and advising possible. Dopamine allows the brain to derive educated guesses about the future from assessing past experiences. This occurs through a partnership with the hippocampus. The hippocampus is wired to detect mismatches between current information and past experience (Kumaran and Duzel 2008). With a healthy flow of dopamine, the aging brain has a greater sense of pattern recognition, which can assist older adults in identifying likely outcomes. In other words, an older adult's hunch regarding a particular circumstance is more likely to be accurate than a younger adult's. Wisdom of this sort is important for intergenerational relationships and helps older adults to guide younger adults in deciding proper action (Kumaran and Duzel 2008).

Acetylcholine

Creative self-expression can provide feelings of gratification through the production of acetylcholine, which is associated with greater brain speed. When acetylcholine levels are balanced, an older adult's brain operates quickly, with optimal creativity and confidence. As with serotonin, this promotes neurogenesis and learning. Acetylcholine facilitates innovation, flexibility, and sociability. Gamma brain waves, which may correspond with acetylcholine, produce a brain state that is maximally sensitive and offer enhanced information-processing speed.

Gamma brain waves and measurable levels of acetylcholine are linked to feelings of inspiration and interconnectedness as well as peak concentration and optimal cognitive functioning. Acetylcholine promotes feelings of being in the "zone." Compassion is also a characteristic brought on by gamma states. Acetylcholine engages the brain at its highest level and motivates older adults to explore ways to use strengths in the service of others, and those others are usually their families or communities.

To promote gamma brain wave states and acetylcholine, a creative professional may encourage an older adult to use what was learned in session with a younger family member at home; for example, the older adult may teach the younger family member how to make a mandala. The older adult may be encouraged to go home and create a mandala alongside a grandchild, for example. Perhaps the older adult's mandala would be based on feelings and color choices that illustrate the love and affection he or she feels for the grandchild. Likewise, perhaps the grandchild's mandala could also express love and affection. This would provide the opportunity for two family members to feel mutually interconnected while also producing a work of art that can be shared with others and displayed within the home to honor the experience. Acetylcholine promotes socialization, and a directive of this sort would facilitate meaningful interpersonal interaction.

Table 2.5 Acetylcholine and creativity

Acetylcholine factor	Creative directive promoting factor
Memory	Remember the steps involved with making a mandala
Confidence	Teach someone else to create a mandala
Attention	Pay attention to the message conveyed through the mandala
Sociability	Communicate and work in tandem with a family member

Like most people, older adults benefit from the opportunity to feel part of a group and to grow and develop within social atmospheres. Interpersonal relationships promote "aha!" moments, breakthroughs, and progression to new, higher levels of performance. Through promoting acetylcholine and gamma states, a creative professional can facilitate an older adult in reaching peak level of attentiveness to new concepts and social connections.

Making art that expresses and enhances mood

Having discussed how the brain processes happiness and how art-making can promote feelings of happiness, I'd like to focus on how visual art elements can stimulate cognitive and emotional functioning. By understanding brain chemistry, creative professionals have the opportunity to positively influence it.

As a creative professional, you can use the art of older adults to understand them and to seek out increasingly beneficial ways for them to express their feelings and thoughts. Please note that when I say that you can use the art to understand the older adult, I am not saying that the artwork will speak for the older adult. For the purposes of this book, I do not suggest that creative professionals attempt to "read" the artwork. What I do suggest is that creative professionals engage the older adult in discussions about the visual elements in the work that may reflect mood and thoughts. In order to do this, a creative professional should be familiar with visual elements in art and be prepared to initiate conversations about those elements.

Visual elements, cognition, and mood

Visual elements are the foundation of form and content in art; they include (but are not limited to) line, color, shape, and space. Through a combination of visual elements, balance, rhythm, contrast, emphasis, and other compositional devices, a person can express and/or elicit moods, memories, or ideas (Malchiodi 2006; Rush 1987). Even the expression of a negative sentiment has the potential to heighten mood through the release of pent-up feelings that may have created a sense of isolation. Additionally, an older adult may view a work of art and find that the external image mirrors their internal state. This may lead to the older adult feeling emotionally validated, and believing that the work of art is an expression of their own emotions whether or not they were the artist.

The ability to connect visual elements to mood is an intrinsic aspect of cognitive functioning and the basis of aesthetic appreciation (Jolley and Thomas 1995). During art-making, the selection of artistic elements affirms the sovereignty of the mind in that the artist has the freedom to manipulate the visual elements to correspond with their own subtle states of mind (Schapiro 1937). The following section describes ways that older adults can be taught to use artistic elements to elevate their own mood and stimulate their cognitive functioning.

COLOR

Creative self-expression through art-making often involves combining colors based on decisions, preferences, mood, and emotional responses. In sessions, older adults select, use, and combine variations of colors that are found on a traditional color wheel, based on the primary colors red, yellow, and blue. The colors red, yellow, and blue have been researched in terms of their associations and subsequent effect on cognition and emotions (Labrecque and Milne 2012; Mehta and Zhu 2009).

Research shows that people cross-culturally tend to choose color–emotion pairings (Labrecque and Milne 2012). "Warm" colors, such as red, have been shown to stimulate dopamine-related feelings such as excitement which is associated with beta waves; in contrast, "cool" colors such as blue have been shown to stimulate feelings such as meditative relaxation which may be associated with serotonin/ alpha brain wave related states (Ueda *et al.* 2004; Yoto *et al.* 2007). Yellow is said to be a "mind-color" that can stimulate the intellect and may be associated with speed of thought; a state which is found with the neurotransmitter acetylcholine and gamma brain waves (Ueda *et al.* 2004).

Color has a profound impact on the brain. The areas of the nervous system that are responsible for emotional arousal are affected as soon as a color is perceived (Zock and Rapp 2010). Decades of research show that color and mood are strongly linked, and this research has given insight into centuries-old practices of ancient cultures, including the Egyptians and Chinese, that relied upon chromotherapy/color therapy, or the practice of using colors to help people feel better (Lichtenfeld *et al.* 2012).

Color therapy is still in practice today in acupuncture clinics, and is based on the belief that there is an associated wavelength, frequency, and quantity of energy for each visible color on the spectrum (Azeemi and Raza 2005). According to chromotherapy theories, colors are said to generate electrical impulses that correspond with biochemical and electrochemical processes within the brain (Azeemi and Raza 2005). Advocates of chromotherapy propose that an electric charge is produced by the frequency and wavelength of colors and affects the brain; this electric charge results in distinct thoughts and mood states (Azeemi and Raza 2005).

Color is a fundamental aspect of human perception, and it influences cognition and mood. Some researchers believe that there is a color for every mode of thought (Mehta and Zhu 2009). Color affects performance on cognitive tasks such as memory, and different colors elicit different cognitive skills (Mehta and Zhu 2009).

In previous research studies, red has shown to elicit cognitive skills that proved helpful in tasks requiring attention and/or problem solving (e.g. memorizing important information or understanding the side effects of a new drug; Mehta and Zhu 2009). Blue elicited cognitive skills that aid exploration, risk-taking, and imagination (e.g. brainstorming session). In other words, individuals exposed to red were better able to recall details, while individuals exposed to blue were better able to come up with novel ideas (Mehta and Zhu 2009).

Teaching older adults to self-stimulate using color when art-making may be beneficial during sessions targeting improved memory. Color is dynamic and the frequency, wavelength, and electrical energy of colors vary by hue, value, and saturation. A color is identified by its hue (yellow, blue, red); saturation refers to how vivid the pigment is (e.g. low saturation makes colors look gray or washed out), and value refers to the amount of lightness (high value) or darkness (low value) present. High saturation increases arousal and excitement, and high value decreases arousal and excitement (Labrecque and Milne 2012).

LINES

Line is the visual element created when depicting a path of a moving point; lines can be short or long, straight or curved, thick or thin, hard or soft (Rush 1987). Lines are a cognitive construct: they do not occur naturally in nature (Rush 1987). The human eye perceives the edges, or "lines," of objects because of a contrast in value or color.

Lines suggest direction, motion, and energy, and they can control the movement of a viewer's eyes across a piece of artwork (Bang 1991). This is why lines have the potential to be a source of both cognitive stimulation and emotional stimulation. By directing the eyes in a specific way, the artwork can take on a narrative or story which may relate to life events and experiences (Malchiodi 2006).

There are five main types of lines: vertical, horizontal, diagonal, curved, and zigzag (Bang 1991). Different kinds of lines can produce different expressive effects: simply speaking, some believe that straight lines are rigid, diagonal lines are exciting, horizontal lines are restful, vertical lines are dignified, and undulating lines are energetic (Rush 1987). Beyond line type, lines can also have qualities such as curves, and angles: curves are said to be serene, graceful, and tender—even sentimental; angles are said to be robust, vigorous, and somewhat more dignified (Hevner 1935). Depending on the line type and quality, lines can elicit relaxed states (alpha waves and serotonin), excited states (beta waves and dopamine), or feelings of inspiration (gamma waves and acetylcholine). Table 2.6 outlines theoretical characteristics of different types of lines more thoroughly (Bang 1991).

The quality of the line is also said to have a symbolic impact. For instance, thick lines may signify exertion, boldness, strength, and hostility, while thin lines may denote more ephemeral qualities and even uncertainty (Bang 1991). Fuzzy diagonal lines may suggest dreaminess or mystery, while jagged horizontal lines may suggest destruction or danger (Bang 1991). Using this information or their own intuition, older adults can begin to express their feelings in concrete and visual ways.

Table 2.6 Line type, associations, effect

Line type	Research-based associated characteristics	Possible neurological effect
Vertical	Strength, potential energy, religiosity	Acetylcholine; gamma
Horizontal	Comfort, relaxation, stability, absence of conflict, peace, security	Serotonin; alpha
Diagonal	Restlessness, movement (either rising or falling), tension, excitement	Dopamine; beta
Curved	The less active the curve the calmer the feeling; gracefulness, softness	Serotonin; alpha
Zigzag	Confusion, excitement, nervousness, anxiety	Dopamine; beta

SHAPE AND SPACE

Shapes are enclosed areas that define an object; they are formed where lines join and intersect and where areas of color meet (Bang 1991). Different shapes have the potential to elicit different moods depending upon the lines and colors used (Bang 1991). Shapes can be classified into two broad categories: organic and geometrical. Organic shapes (e.g. circles, ovals) are said to be pleasing, natural, and comfortable to view; thus possibly eliciting alpha brain waves and serotonin responses. In contrast, geometrical shapes (e.g. squares, triangles, rectangles) are associated with complexity, stability, assertion, and severity, and may elicit dopamine responses or beta brain wave states.

Space refers to the area (either 2-D or 3-D) within, around, between, above, or below the objects depicted (Bang 1991). Positive spaces are those that are occupied by shapes or forms and negative spaces are the emptiness within or surrounding the shapes or forms (Bang 1991). The locations of the objects and the amount of both positive and negative space are associated with feelings and moods. Table 2.7 outlines those associations. Whereas objects located on the bottom half of the page may provide a feeling of being more grounded, objects in the upper half of the page may provide the feeling of being freer, lighter, and happier. These feelings may correspond with neurological states that affect cognitive and emotional functioning.

Table 2.7 Space occupied, associations, effect

Space occupied	Research-based associations	Possible neurological effect
Bottom half of picture	Objects feel more grounded, more attached to the earth	Serotonin; alpha
Center of page	Center of attention, point of greatest attraction; focus	Dopamine; beta
Upper half of picture	Feeling of being lighter and happier, freer, triumphant, spiritual	Acetylcholine; gamma

Combining visual elements for enhanced mood

One simple means of combining all of these visual elements without increasing stress or self-consciousness is doodling based on intuition and impulse. Doodling is a form of expression that incorporates lines, colors, shapes, and space usage into an intuitive process of creating (Goldschmidt 2003). Doodling is an activity that is self-paced and repetitive; it doesn't require pre-defined skill or controlled processing, such as performance monitoring or inhibition (Andrade 2010).

Doodling has been shown to enhance cognitive performance and memory by aiding concentration (Dalebroux, Goldstein, and Winner 2008). Depressive ruminations and worry depend upon a mind that is lingering on saddening internal stimuli and unable to concentrate on external stimuli (Smallwood, McSpadden, and Schooler 2007). Although narrative drawings or drawings that portray a coherent story can provide a form of venting, doodles tend to depict more positive emotions or distracting content. Creating a drawing that expresses a current mood (venting) is less effective for improving mood than creating a drawing that depicts something happy or that allows the mind to concentrate on neutral, relaxing external stimuli (Dalebroux *et al.* 2008).

When venting through a narrative work, an older adult may express negative emotions; however, when fantasizing and simply doodling, an older adult may imagine forms and visual elements that prompt positive emotions (Dalebroux *et al.* 2008). Although both may boost mood, the latter has shown to be more beneficial (Dalebroux *et al.* 2008). Creating a work of art which expresses positive emotions results in a more positive emotional state (Dalebroux *et al.* 2008).

Art-making in groups for enhanced mood

Although art-making alone can enhance mood and stimulate cognition, making art in social settings intensifies these positive effects. Time and again, social support has been found to be the strongest predictor of positive moods and happiness in late-life (Lu 1999). This is because social support allows older adults to experience interpersonal trust, one of the strongest factors linked to happiness (Lu 1999).

During difficult phases in life, older adults may feel out of touch with their emotions. Allowing older adults to equate emotions to artistic elements may promote expressivity, decrease feelings of isolation, and increase the potential for socially meaningful interaction. This ultimately leads to enhanced mood.

Figure 2.6 illustrates this progression, starting with the upper left quadrant. First, an idea, thought, or emotion creates an impetus for creativity and illuminates an individual's inner world, stimulating brain states associated with creativity (alpha waves and serotonin). Second, that inspiration and vision is expressed within an aesthetic product (e.g. a painting), stimulating brain states associated with achievement and focus (beta waves and dopamine). Third, the aesthetic product may be presented to the group and perhaps the larger community (e.g. galleries, museums, newspapers, magazines, and websites), yielding increases in socialization and corresponding brain states (gamma waves and acetylcholine). Finally, the artwork may undergo a public or group interpretation of its meaning, potentially influencing each viewer's world view or emotional state and thus stimulating their cognitive states positively (Grey 2013).

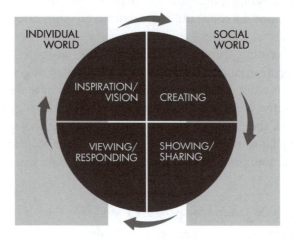

Figure 2.6 Quadrants

In my doctoral research, clients valued highly the socialization during cognitive training sessions and named the social component as one of the most influential aspects of art therapy (Alders 2012). The following poem, written by my clients as a group at the closing of a quilt-making session, demonstrates the value placed on social interactions.

Not Alone
It takes many pieces all together
We all helped each other
Better to work together than alone

The physical face-to-face encounters during creative sessions allow for older adults to share feelings, experiences, values, skills, and self-expression styles. For most older adults, meaningful socializing may be a preferable approach to memory training (Alders 2012). By building on strengths, creative activity like art-making has been shown to reduce depression and isolation, offering the power of choice and decisions (Hannemann 2006).

The creation of artwork in social settings may provide a neurological reward that has the potential to flood the brain with dopamine, promoting neuroplasticity and thus aiding memory. The reward can be intra-personal in that the older adult may feel a sense of accomplishment, and the reward may be inter-personal in that peers, family, and community members acknowledge the achievement of creativity. For a reward to effectively motivate older adults to do their best, the reward must come soon after the artwork has been completed. Providing creative sessions in a group setting increases the likelihood that an older adult will experience social rewards for their creativity in the form of acknowledgements, praise, and more.

In creative sessions, social interaction may promote interdependence. Interdependence occurs when there is cooperation rather than competition. Much like in other stages of life, older adults may feel competitive with one another to create the best work of art; this is another instance where a creative professional, knowledgeable in the importance of process over product, can intervene. When older adults create artwork with unfamiliar materials, they may compare their works to others' and be negatively impacted emotionally. They may form the impression that they are not performing "up to par," even though their products are not true reflections of their abilities.

The process of making the artwork is the stimulus for enhanced cognitive performance. Creativity-based memory training is a therapeutic process rather than a recreational activity. So the focus of each older adult should be on their own process of creating, and their own personal response to the colors, lines, and textures they are creating.

Social equality vs. stratification during creativity and happiness

Regardless of age, human behavior follows tendencies of a subtle (and, sometimes, not so subtle) social hierarchy, known as stratification: the hierarchical positioning of people based on gender, race, and/or socio-economic factors (Verdugo 2009). Social hierarchy affects dopamine levels and can affect an older adult's ability to feel happy and content in a group setting. No one wants to feel like they are not welcome or experience discrimination. Feelings of equality and mutual respect are essential to promoting optimal brain states and feelings of pleasure, enjoyment, and comfort during cognitive training. Experiencing joy requires feeling accepted and appreciated (Martinez *et al.* 2010).

In today's quickly diversifying and aging world, homogenous groups are less and less prevalent. Instead, diverse and multicultural groups are the reality. Creative professionals will encounter older adults from an array of ethnicities and cultures. Racism and socio-economic class discrimination may occur during the creative session, and both have been found to contribute to higher levels of stress and depressed mood, which negatively affect memory (Turner and Avison 2003).

If a creative professional aims to improve older adult memory through enhancing mood, cognitive stimulation, and socialization, they must create settings where there are equal opportunities for social interaction regardless of background. Creative professionals must set boundaries and facilitate appropriate interaction as well as break down barriers between older adults by encouraging interaction through the artwork, using it as a mediator for discussions.

My previous research demonstrated that, despite initial discrimination, gains in mutual respect and interpersonal trust occurred when boundaries were set by therapists (Alders 2012). Below is an excerpt from the clinical notes for a Haitian/black female older adult, "M," who initially endured, and ultimately overcame, continuous open discrimination by the Latino/Hispanic clients. Toward the end of a ten-week expressive memory program, M began to use her art to demonstrate self-worth and positive mood, and she proudly paraded her artwork around the Latino group members. The following includes excerpts from multiple notes regarding my sessions (Alders 2012):

> FIRST SESSION: Inter-group discrimination by ethnicity and socioeconomic status could be noted and was immediately redirected … SECOND SESSION: M, a Haitian client, repeatedly described feeling discriminated against for being Black. M explained that she would work in the art therapy groups, but not with the "white people" [a reference to the Caucasian Latinos] … THIRD SESSION: After completing her work, M approached the Caucasian Latino group and proudly showed her artwork. She walked around so that each "White" member could see what she had made. She smiled and self-praised in front of the Latino members; she received sincere praise and positive feedback from several Latino group members in return. The Latino participants praised her talent. FOURTH

SESSION: Several Latino clients chose to sit with M at the table where she normally sits by herself. They initiated conversation about M's work and she could be seen smiling and laughing.

Whether poor or rich, privileged or underprivileged, all societies have one commonality: the presence of art (Anderson and Milbrandt 2005). Art serves a distinct social role: it can overturn destructive social systems, promote group unity, and enhance interpersonal trust (Alba and Islam 2009; Craig and Paraiso 2009). This ultimately serves to promote feelings of happiness and social support, thereby creating optimal brain states for improved memory.

Summary

Mood can affect cognitive functioning for better or worse. During creative self-expression, older adults have the opportunity to focus on positive emotions and experiences while also engaging in rewarding interaction with others. Diverse groups of older adults may result in discrimination occurring during creativity-based memory training. However, when respect is prioritized by a creative professional, the older adults will respond to the modeled behavior.

The following chapter outlines ways to encourage therapeutic interaction during art-making. Inter-group dynamics during creativity-based memory training will be described. Specifically, Chapter 3 outlines ways of using art to both stimulate memory and incorporate culture into sessions in ways that achieve therapeutic socialization.

CULTURE, COMMUNICATION, AND ART

KEY CONCEPT: Culture affects communication and therefore self-expression during social art-making.

WORDBANK
(Definitions can be found throughout the chapter.)

1	Pragmatic competence		9	Perception/interpretation
2	Assumptive worlds		10	Evaluation/connection
3	De-centering techniques		11	Metamessage
4	Triadic schema		12	Explanatory model
5	Hierarchical inclusion		13	Culture
6	Homogenous group		14	Universality
7	Multicultural sensitivity		15	Visual literacy
8	Sensus communis		16	Figurative expressions

Promoting socialization during memory training

The same neural mechanisms that underlie an older adult's ability to express themselves creatively also controls their ability to function socially, problem solve, and manage emotions (Bar-On *et al.* 2003). The lives and cognitive abilities of older adults are improved through opportunities for creative self-expression because those opportunities stimulate mental, emotional, and social abilities.

This chapter focuses on strategies for enhancing the social interaction among diverse older adults. Socialization is very important for memory training outcomes. A recent study showed that the risk of developing memory loss/Alzheimer's disease was higher for those who reported being lonely (Wilson *et al.* 2007). Increasing social networks provides unique health benefits for older adults (Cornwell, Laumann, and Schumm 2008). The areas of the brain that are engaged during socialization are responsible for working memory, attention, and general cognitive control (Sutcliffe *et al.* 2012). The following statement explains the cognitive stimulation involved during socialization:

> a simple exchange of views between two people requires that they pay attention to each other, maintain in memory the topic of the conversation and respective contributions, adapt to each other's perspective, infer each other's beliefs and desires, assess the situational constraints acting on them at the time, and inhibit irrelevant or inappropriate behavior. (Ybarra *et al.* 2008, p.249)

During sessions, older adults may share personal information and reminiscence during art-making and, as a result, creative professionals may become deeply involved with older adults' lives. As creative professionals get to know older adults, they can help them connect with other older adults in meaningful ways. When older adults are able to connect with others, they have the chance to convey what they value in life. This can make self-expression in social settings exciting and rewarding, especially when it assists older adults with connecting with others. Among the deepest and most sincere of human needs is a need to be socially accepted and to belong. Social interaction is an effective means of reinforcing an older adult's healthy self-image and self-worth.

Socialization promotes optimal cognitive functioning and memory skills by creating an emotionally and mentally stimulating melting pot of different perspectives and relationships (Ybarra *et al.* 2008). That said, socialization can also create a feeling of vulnerability, which can be intimidating. When there is a diverse group of people, it becomes harder to gauge what is socially acceptable. Although this can provoke an even greater level of cognitive stimulation, it can also lead to a sense of uncertainty in terms of what to say and do.

Creative professionals will find that not all older adults want to interact with one another or share personal information. Cultural, socio-economic, educational, religious, and other differences can make older adults uncomfortable with one another. Additionally, some older adults may be socially withdrawn and reluctant to engage in group settings. There is a human tendency to seek out and interact only with people that have similar backgrounds, beliefs, and perspectives (Cornwell *et al.* 2008). This is the safe way to interact because it minimizes the risk for rejection. As a result, as individuals age, their social networks tend to shrink (Cornwell *et al.* 2008). Bypassing older adult tendencies to limit social interaction is important for memory training outcomes.

Because art facilitates communication, it also facilitates relationships. For creative professionals such as therapists, an ethical practice is one that promotes inter-connectedness and a strengthening of social solidarity (Welsch 1999). Art viewing and, particularly, art-making can promote older adult inter-connectedness and social solidarity because it provides a means for allowing private realities and identities to be explored and shared (Malchiodi 2006).

Identity affects relationships and social behavior, and throughout life, identity is continuously reconstructed (Thorsen 1998). Art can become a medium through which the identity is naturally explored (Wilson and Ross 2003). Culture, or the ideas and practices among interconnected individuals, is a major part of identity, and should be a central focus in sessions with diverse older adults (Gutierrez and Rogoff 2003).

Culture

Culture determines how individuals within a culture communicate their thoughts, emotions, and perspectives (Dingfelder 2005; Jones, Chow, and Gatz 2006). This is because culture shapes everything that an individual knows or thinks he or she knows about the world; in other words, culture shapes older adult assumptive worlds (Cann *et al.* 2009; Dimond 1981). An assumptive world is a person's internal model against which present experiences are compared (Cann *et al.* 2009). When one person's assumptive world differs from that of another's, communication and interaction suffers.

How older adults live, how their families function, how free time is spent, and how friendships form are all culturally imbued areas of life (Anderson 1995; Anderson and Milbrandt 2005; Harris 2008). In short, culture shapes the meaning people make of their life (Merriam and Mohamad 2000). Creative professionals are more effective when they understand older adult cultural beliefs (Harris 2008). Understanding cultural beliefs allows professionals to adopt culturally sensitive communication patterns and that is essential in providing culturally competent services (Mahoney *et al.* 2005).

When older adults encounter an unfamiliar situation, such as a group of people from outside of their own culture with differing cultural practices, they may experience culture shock, or feel anxious and disoriented (Mahoney *et al.* 2005). Multicultural group experiences may bring behaviors and interactions into question. People from different cultures interact differently. As a result, identity and self-concept may be challenged. A person may ask themselves, "How am I supposed to be? How am I supposed to act?"

In these cases, creative professionals may find it useful to reinforce older adult behaviors which are socially valued within the group setting. For example, a creative professional may say, "Maria, I noticed that when you were working, several other group members looked to you for ideas. You really took the lead and showed a lot of enthusiasm. Great job!" or "Jon, you seem to be such a thoughtful person. You really considered which colors to choose and which materials to use. Your decisions make your artwork distinctly yours. Wonderful!"

However, a possibly even better approach may be the introduction of art and art-making. Art may be one way to make the social process easier and to assist diverse older adults during interaction and collaboration. In a qualitative study conducted with older adults between 1997 and 2000, the introduction of artwork was found to generate an increase in positive verbal and non-verbal exchange (Hodges, Keeley, and Grier 2001). Throughout the creative process, older adults present and describe their artworks to one another. This requires empathetic listening on the part of the group members, which facilitates interpersonal understanding.

Artistic expression is considered an essential component of cultural identity (Jameson 2006). Throughout history, art has been used to portray a shared identity and promote a sense of belonging among people of diverse cultures (Alders 2010). Asian, African-American, and Latino cultures all incorporate the creation and use of images and pictorial symbolism in highly respected folk healing traditions (Graham *et al.* 2005).

Latino/Hispanic folk artwork often reflects themes of social connections, identity, and cohesive communities, and folk healing practices among Latinos are said to promote a sense of belonging (Comas-Dias 2006). Much of Mexico's public art centers on the idea of *Mexicanidad,* or "Mexicanness" which relates to what it means and how it feels to be Mexican (Franquiz and Brochin-Ceballos 2006). Similarly, African-American folk art within the US is said to establish social status, and Asians have used folk art within their communities in the form of symbolic imagery (e.g. dragons) to ascribe culturally significant meanings (e.g. enhanced health) to images and symbols (Metcafi 2010).

Since art is universally present throughout the world, aesthetic reflection and reasoning appeals to universal reason, or sensus communis (Sartwell 2003). Art serves to present subjective and variable stories that incorporate human experiences shared by all people (e.g. motherhood, loss, isolation, joy, manual labor). Creativity and art-making have shown to enhance multicultural sensitivity and cultural competence (Alders 2012; Cohen 2006; Leung *et al.* 2008). By enhancing creativity, the creative professional has the potential to increase social interaction and enhance cross-cultural understanding (Anderson 1995; Cohen 2006). During art-based memory training sessions, creative professionals may connect older adults with one another by linking artwork to personal cross-cultural experiences. However, in order for this to be a success, older adults must first be open to the idea of having genuine interaction with one another.

Providing cultural neutrality

In a homogenous group, each of the older adults would be similar in age, socio-economic background, culture, and ethnicity; their assumptive worlds would overlap enough so that interaction would comply with one set of behavioral norms. However, a homogenous group is not likely to occur in today's increasingly diverse world. In a normal group setting there are layers of social relationships that represent differences in assumptive worlds; the more differences that exist in assumptions about the world, the less social inclusion, cultural understanding, and social acceptance there is (Sutcliffe *et al.* 2012).

Assumptions about the world shape older adults' explanatory models or how they explain, justify, or rationalize what is happening around them throughout life (Talamantes, Lindeman, and Mouton 2010). When faced with a different culture or unknown circumstance, an individual may realize that he doesn't know how to explain what is happening or what he is witnessing. When an older adult's explanatory model lacks the information needed in a given situation, discomfort arises; his world feels less secure and his assumptions seem less accurate (Talamantes *et al.* 2010).

Most people try their best to avoid this by surrounding themselves with only those people who share a similar explanatory model. This is illustrated in Figure 3.1, in which concentric circles correspond to hierarchical inclusion. Individuals in the center circle would share similar assumptions about the world, and each outward layer represents social groups that are increasingly different in their assumptions (Sutcliffe *et al.* 2011).

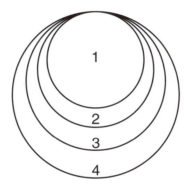

Figure 3.1 Model of social inclusivity by hierarchies

In the center circle, the relationships would be strongest. Those in the center, upper circle would know each other's names, make eye contact (if culturally acceptable), and show physical affection such as greeting with hugs or kisses on the cheek (again, if culturally acceptable). They would likely agree with each other about what is important in life, what is normal in social settings, and how communication occurs.

Because of differences in world view, those in the center, upper circle may not show the same level of affection to those in the second, lower circle. They may know those individuals' names and say hello and make eye contact, but they would not be as close or as willing to disclose emotional content. Likewise, older adults in the center circle may not know the older adults' names in the third and fourth circles. Older adults in the fourth circle and lowest circle may not receive eye contact or be engaged in conversation; they may feel like outsiders, and they may be treated as such by older adults in the center circle.

Figure 3.1 illustrates a situation in which the majority assumptive world became centralized. In this circumstance, a single group's assumptive world and explanatory model becomes the deciding factor for social inclusion. Creative professionals have the opportunity to de-centralize this system through art by setting behavioral standards, promoting social bonds among all the older adults in the group, and by immediately redirecting hierarchical inclusion.

Art facilitates a de-centering process by allowing information and meaning to be communicated on many levels (Dewey 1957). Creative interaction is marked by dynamic communication, multifaceted connections among ideas, and numerous meaningful solutions to problems; creativity encourages flexible thinking, which enhances multicultural understanding (Anderson 1995; Anderson and Milbrandt 2005; Dewey 1957).

De-centering techniques may eliminate hierarchical inclusion and enhance members' interest in one another by allowing art-based routines (e.g. making, viewing, and discussing) to take precedence. In this way, art becomes the center of the social process (as illustrated in Figure 3.2) and can build rapport and communication, therefore assisting with memory-training goals (Talamantes *et al.* 2010). As all participants engage in the same pursuit, art-making equalizes behavioral norms. Additionally, when older adults show respect and appreciation for each other's artwork they are simultaneously showing respect for each other's assumptive world. Artwork that connects to personal experiences and world views represents assumptive worlds and explanatory models.

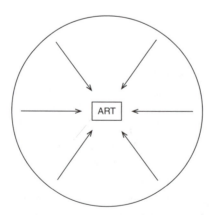

Figure 3.2 Art as the center of the social process

In a practical sense, creative professionals can employ de-centering techniques by using a schedule that emphasizes artwork and art-making in each session. For example:

1. Begin with a discussion or selection of a life event that will provide the inspiration for the session's art-making.

2. Follow with a period of concentrated effort in art-making.

3. Proceed with a display of the artwork created.

4. End with a discussion of the group's art-making and experiences during the creative session.

Such a routine will put the focus of the session on the art, which decreases opportunities for hierarchical inclusion. Additionally, by creating universal opportunities for sharing and attention, participants are required to distribute group status equally rather than according to outside factors such as education, wealth, or country of origin.

In addition to establishing a routine, creative professionals can implement standards to promote interconnectivity. The clearer the standards are for socially acceptable behavior, the more likely interpersonal interaction will be enhanced. Clear standards promote strong relationships, and the stronger the relationships are between the older adults and the creative professional, the more likely the memory training will be effective. Additionally, if older adults are encouraged to be friendly to one another, the atmosphere will be relaxed and comfortable, which encourages self-expression. The following list contains examples of rules that may promote interdependence and support among older adults; this very list could be printed and posted in the location that hosts group sessions.

Examples of rules that may promote positive outcomes with older adults

1. Arrive to group on time.

2. Seating is assigned to promote training outcomes.

3. Know and use each member's name.

4. Physical affection should be shown universally to all members or not at all.

5. Be able to identify at least one commonality you share with each member.

6. Avoid arguments; put the relationship first and agree to disagree, if necessary.

7. Provide praise to one another.

8. Ask questions about each other's artwork.

9. Show interest in one another's accomplishments.

10. Focus on cooperation rather than competition; learn from each other and teach each other.

Communication

Communication connects older adults to one another and to the greater community. Fear of miscommunication can limit older adults in their level of comfort during interaction.

Saying something inappropriately or at an inappropriate time can have a greater impact on communication than even grammatical inaccuracy (Harris 2008; Kasper and Dahl 1991). Being able to express and communicate ideas as intended, and in a way that promotes positive social interaction, is referred to as pragmatic competence (Barron and Warga 2007; Harris 2008). In group settings, and especially when describing emotional experiences, pragmatic competence is difficult to achieve regardless of age, culture, and circumstance. That difficulty is often compounded among a group of older adult individuals from a mix of cultural and socio-economic backgrounds.

Language use becomes increasingly complex with age, and creative professionals would be well advised to consider communication trends relevant to late-life. For instance, children tend to rely on more concrete uses of language, but older adults use more figurative (and culturally idiomatic) language (Vulchanova, Vulchanov, and Stankova 2011). Some social constructs (e.g. figurative language or metaphors) vary so much across cultures that words and communication become irrelevant.

Verbal communication may be misunderstood due to errors in translation, context, tone, or word choice. Research shows that over 65 percent of social meaning is conveyed through non-verbal clues, and some psychologists claim that non-verbal communication provides up to 90 percent of the metamessage, or underlying meaning (Harris 2008). The metamessage encompasses the purpose of communication and affects what is interpreted by the listener (Barron and Warga 2007; Harris 2008).

Metamessages are often based on emotion and, because of this, emotion is a crucial aspect of communication (Horlings 2008). Artwork can prioritize the metamessage by emphasizing the emotional content and making it tangible. As a result, artwork can promote successful pragmatic competence.

When miscommunication occurs between two people, it is often the emotional content that is misunderstood; the listener's interpretation may not accurately reflect the intention or feelings of the speaker. At the same time, when a person describes an emotional experience, he or she may not immediately know if that description has been understood; this creates vulnerability.

Emotions are subjective experiences that are often difficult to capture in literal terms (Vulchanova *et al.* 2011). Some emotions are incommunicable without figurative language like metaphors and idioms; figurative expressions help to capture the essence of an emotional experience (Henley 2000). The more intense and complex an emotion is, the more figurative the language is in communication (Geary 2011).

Individuals from differing cultures may not understand each other's use of figurative language, and this creates an "in group" and an "out group." Figurative expressions cannot be translated directly and are difficult for non-native speakers to grasp. For instance, someone may use the phrase "freaking out" to describe intense anxiety, or "warm and fuzzy" to describe being happy. Likewise, "hollow" may be used to describe deep sadness. These phrases don't lend themselves to cross-cultural understanding.

Figurative expressions are easier to understand when they are illustrated in imagery (Henley 2000). In fact, creative professionals can center entire sessions on the imagery related to figurative language. The idiom is one form of figurative language that lends itself to imagery because its literal meaning doesn't have universality, or cultural cross-over. An idiom is a group of words that has a meaning that isn't deducible from the individual words (e.g. raining cats and dogs).

Using idioms in sessions can be therapeutic. For instance, asking, "What does it mean to say that something is the 'apple of my eye'?" can lead to a discussion about possible meanings and provide opportunities for group problem-solving. In this way, the same idiomatic material that can create problems in communication can become a positive focus for social and emotional art-making (Henley 2000). Figurative language, like idioms, can give insight into culture, stretch abstract thinking capacities, and provide a distinct source of mental stimulation (Henley 2000). Table 3.1 outlines some examples of figurative expressions that have idiomatic equivalents in English, Spanish, and Chinese. Expressions such as these may prompt dialogue, inspire images, or promote cultural understanding.

Table 3.1 Idiomatic equivalents

English	Spanish	Chinese
Birds of a feather flock together	Tell me with whom you walk and I'll tell you who you are. (*Dime con quien andas y te dire quien eres.*)	Similar things are categorized together. (物以类聚 *wù yǐ lèijù*)
Practice makes perfect	Only if you practice something, will you be an expert, a master. (*El ejercicio hace al maestro.*)	Experience can give way to skill. (熟能生巧 *shú néng shēng qiǎo*)
The first step is the hardest	The longest journey is that which begins with a first step. (*El viaje más largo es el que comienza con el primer paso.*)	The first step in a thousand different matters is always difficult. (万事起头难 *wànshì qǐtóu nán*)
Rome was not built in a day	Zamora was not won in an hour. (*No se ganó Zamora en una hora.*) Zamora = town in Spain; battle	Three feet of ice is not the result of one cold day. (冰冻三尺，非一日之寒 *bīng dòng sān chǐ, fēi yī rì zhī hán*)
A friend in need is a friend indeed	In danger the friend is met. (*En el peligro se conoce el amigo.*)	In adversity, true feelings are revealed. (患难见真情 *huànnàn jiàn zhēnqíng*)

The metaphor is another form of figurative language that incorporates symbolic meaning. A metaphor is a figure of speech that designates one thing as another to make an implicit comparison (e.g. life is a breeze).

Metaphors evoke a rich range of verbal and sensory associations and open up new possibilities of behavior and thought (Geary 2011). Interestingly, the brain often confuses literal and metaphoric content and processes the information in the same way (Sapolsky 2010). This "neural confusion" gives symbols enormous power; the use of metaphors and other strategies can increase learning retention by as much as 40 percent (Sapolsky 2010).

Many languages are full of metaphors, and research on the English language suggests that one metaphor is uttered for every 10 to 25 words, or about six metaphors a minute (Geary 2011). Metaphorical language may facilitate the communication of intense emotional experiences. Metaphors are often used to describe subjective feelings and some theories claim that metaphors create a sense of emotional closeness between the speaker and the listener (Geary 2011). For the creative professional, this means that figurative language like metaphors are very valuable, as long as they are cross-culturally understood.

Metaphors can be represented in both written and visual forms. One way in which art is capable of metaphor is through the incorporation of color. There are emotional and symbolic associations with different colors, and daily speech frequently incorporates the use of colors to increase expressiveness (e.g. feeling blue). In some cultures, the color black may to refer to a depressed mood, and the color pink may have a positive connotation (e.g. to see through rose-colored glasses), referencing optimism and happiness (Zock and Rapp 2010). However, associations to colors may vary and discussing what color means is in itself a culturally sensitive metaphoric discussion.

Art in communication

Art serves as a means for older adults to communicate with one another around issues of culture and identity. Culturally imbued concepts can be conveyed through images, but art is more than a mere substitute for language. In therapeutic sessions, art can function as both a symbol for communication and an intermediary device that facilitates communication; in this way, art allows for an alternation between non-verbal and verbal communication (Morrell 2011).

Art symbols can serve as metaphors to represent strong emotions that may otherwise be incommunicable, and also serves as a way to express and explore those feelings. Art has the potential to become a staging ground where connections are made and ideas are integrated (Morrell 2011). Whereas a particular feeling may be hard to verbally express and may require verbose, time-consuming explanations in an attempt to do so, a work of art becomes a single representation of that attempt. Unlike verbal language, concrete works of art can be directly manipulated to better illustrate an implied meaning (Morrell 2011). An older adult can continually rework their image until it represents and contains the emotional impact desired.

The employment of visual imagery fosters a growing understanding of people, emotions, and personal circumstances (Gallos 2008). When communicating in sessions, creative professionals and older adults can refer back to a concrete representation, which can provide a point of reference that mediates discussions (Malchiodi 2006; Morrell 2011). This specific use of imagery as both a point of reference during verbal communication and a symbol for what is communicated can provide a safe means of expressing emotion because it lowers the likelihood of miscommunication within culturally diverse groups.

Art, when used for expressive purposes, takes on a triadic schema (i.e. the viewer, the creator/creative process, and the product; Morrell 2011; Spendlove 2007). This triadic schema can assist older adults in communicating and socializing with others in meaningful ways, and is illustrated in Figure 3.3 (Morrell 2011; Spendlove 2007). Rather than verbally communicating ideas that are culturally misunderstood and maybe even opposing, two older adults can come together to view a work of art and discuss what they see and what they interpret that to mean. The artwork itself creates a third item in the interaction since that is where both older adults' attention is directed. The older adults describe what they see and find a means of mutually understanding what is being portrayed.

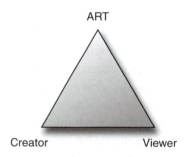

Figure 3.3 Triadic schema

Visual literacy

Looking at art and attempting to understand the portrayed meaning is an exercise in visual literacy. Before the 21st century, the term literate referred almost exclusively to a person's ability to read and write, and that label separated the educated from the uneducated (Chauvin 2003). This definition of literacy is now outdated, because literacy has adopted an additional meaning: one which involves visual competencies such as the ability to integrate sensory input, categorically sort it, and then interpret the content of multiple components of an image simultaneously (Chauvin 2003).

Visual literacy can be defined as both the ability to recognize and understand ideas conveyed through images (e.g. art viewing) and the ability to convey ideas or messages through imagery (e.g. art-making; Aanstoos 2003). The concept of visual literacy is based on the idea that visual images can act as a language (Aanstoos 2003). Visual literacy requires a process of taking in information from the world through the senses and comparing new information with what has already been stored in the brain in schemata patterns and representations (Anderson and Milbrandt 2005; Pauwels 2008; Schunk 2007). By providing a means for visual literacy, art communicates information that may otherwise be misunderstood if that content were to be only communicated verbally. Because visual literacy plays a role in the non-verbal transference of information (Arnheim 2004) older adults can use art to understand one another's ideas, experiences, and feelings.

Processing visual meaning requires inductive reasoning; older adults must be able to attribute meaning to the symbols and abstract information found within the art. Some may say that humans are biologically wired to do just that, considering that the visual cortex (the area of the brain responsible for processing visual images) is the largest system within the brain (Arnheim 2004).

Like words, images are context-sensitive (Anderson and Milbrandt 2005). This context enables the development of the metaphor. The ability to understand metaphor, verbal or non-verbal, is the crux of creativity (Anderson and Milbrandt 2005). Visual metaphors create a multifocal symbolic message; in other words, visual metaphor enables images to communicate on multiple levels simultaneously while compressing and intensifying information; this allows for a concentration of meaning (Anderson and Milbrandt 2005).

Throughout history, individuals have communicated with one another using art as a means to visually code complex social concepts in elaborate metaphors. Because of this, the creation of art may be a culturally inclusive, non-traditional approach to providing cognitive stimulation. Educational, historical, cultural, and other contextual factors do not rule out "neural processes that arise in the empathetic understanding of visual artworks" (Freedberg and Gallese 2007, p.197).

Humans have created images to convey meaning for thousands of years, and human capacity for thought is inextricably linked to images (Felten 2008). On a biological level, the information-processing system includes distinct and complex dual neural channels for visual and pictorial processing (Felten 2008). Research demonstrates that seeing is not simply a process of passive reception of stimuli: it also involves an active construction of meaning as well as a personal interpretation (Felten 2008).

Social sharing of meaning through art

Some may assume that the ability to understand non-verbal messages in imagery requires prior training or special skills. However, this is not the case. Unless impeded by a physical or neurological disability, humans are equipped with the capacity for visual cognition (Felten 2008). Additionally, an image's lack of fidelity to visual reality doesn't necessarily impede a viewer's ability to interpret the content, even if that viewer is inexperienced (Messaris 1993). Generally speaking, visual literacy is a universal and cross-cultural skill. No specific training is required on the part of the viewer or the artist for meaning to be conveyed. In fact, some art therapists believe that artistic skill can actually impede authentic, raw, emotional meaning in art from being conveyed (Malchiodi 2006).

Creative professionals can facilitate a group exploration of the meaning in visual images by asking older adults strategic questions about aspects of the art products. Questions such as "What do you see in this image? What might this image mean?" may encourage a higher degree of respect for diverse perspectives as older adults explain the different components of the image that they see and the different meanings that they interpret.

To increase socialization and promote effective communication through art, creative professionals will benefit from addressing the key elements underlining interaction through artwork: perception (what do you see?), interpretation (what do I/we think of what you see?), and evaluation/connection (how does this relate to my/our life?).

Perception

The development of art throughout human history represents an instinctual need to perceive reality concretely (Campbell 1999). That is why the appreciation of a work of art is guided by the cognitive ability of perception. A major function of making art is to explore information and this is an extension of the brain's most basic perceptive purpose. At its most fundamental level, cognitive performance is simply a range of mental operations that enable the accurate perception of incoming information (Alzheimer's Association 2010b). Because perception is influenced by culture, the accuracy of perceptions can be debated by those of differing cultural viewpoints.

Visual art contributes to cognitive abilities because it allows for perceptual exploration. During a session, perception can be explored within a group through an analysis and discussion of the elements of a work of art (e.g. color, line, shape, and space). Thus the art piece becomes a vehicle for sharing world views: "This is what I see. This is what I think it means." This process of creative interaction, dynamic communication, and multifaceted connections among ideas gives rise to meaningful problem solving and flexible thinking (Anderson 1995; Anderson and Milbrandt 2005; Dewey 1957).

The following questions can encourage older adults' perceptual abilities during a session (adapted from Anderson and Milbrandt 2005).

1. What do you see?

2. What types of colors/shapes/lines/space are present?

3. What artistic characteristics are present (e.g. contrast, balance, movement, negative space, textures)?

4. Is there a focal point in the artwork? What is it? What causes you to look there?

5. Does the artwork reveal any cultural information about the artist?

Interpretation

Culture is a form of acquired knowledge that is used to interpret experiences (Harris 2008). An interpretation of artwork brings culture into the foreground during a session. As each older adult provides a unique interpretation of the artwork, different perspectives can be shared in a way that influences the group as a whole. Through interpretation, older adults seek to understand what a work of art is expressing. Rather than relying on description and observation (as perception does), interpretation relies on reasoning.

Information such as the subject matter of the work can be described in a session in order to understand deeper levels of meaning (e.g. "There appears to be a young girl on a bike"). Through this process, older adults can consider a variety of factors such as autobiographical aspects (e.g. did the artist portray something that relates to his life?), history (e.g. is this a life experience that you witnessed in your community growing up?), personal experiences of the viewer (e.g. does this show something that you've personally experienced?), and other social and cultural factors (Anderson and Milbrandt 2005).

Art serves to seize meaning and embody it (Alexander 1999; Sartwell 2003). However, previous life experiences play a critical role in an older adult's interpretation of meaning in art; for this reason, meaning will constantly slip in and out of definitiveness and therefore lends itself to the influence of others' insights (Radford and Radford 2005). This is why group discussions regarding perception and interpretation are stimulating on cognitive, emotional, and social levels.

The following questions can encourage older adults' interpretative abilities during a session (adapted from Anderson and Milbrandt 2005).

1. What title would you give this work if you were the artist?

2. What do you think this work means?

3. What mood is presented in the image?

4. If you were inside the work as a particular character, form, or figure, what would you be thinking and feeling?

5. What message does this artwork express?

Evaluation and connection

Evaluation requires an older adult to explore what is valued in a particular work of art. Generally speaking, the qualities that a viewer values in art are often the same qualities that he or she values in life; hence, the evaluation of art is highly subjective. Through evaluation, older adults can decide whether or not an artwork relates to their past experiences and to what they find meaningful in life. This relationship between art, life, and what is valued underlies why art and visual culture tend to address significant life experiences, such as relationships and feelings (Anderson 1995).

Following a process of evaluation, older adults have the potential to make connections with the life experiences being portrayed, and therefore with the concerns of the community and other group members. Art can be used to understand universal human concerns, to express the concerns of particular people in a particular time and place, and to express the concerns and values of a particular person. As older adults compare life experiences and relate the significance of those experiences to the artwork, the art enables a re-evaluation of important aspects of interaction and can heighten levels of compassion (Anderson and Milbrandt 2005).

If a viewer evaluates a work of art highly, that viewer probably relates personally to the reconstructed reality portrayed within the art (Dewey 1957). For this reason, visual art has been described as a "smooth operational surface of communication" with the "self" or society at large (Baudrillard 1983, pp.127–8 as cited in Radford and Radford 2005). If art successfully communicates with the viewer, then it sparks an internal and external connection, which is the basis of healthy socialization.

The following questions can encourage older adults' evaluation and connecting abilities during a session (adapted from Anderson and Milbrandt 2005):

1. How does this work make you feel?

2. What does this work make you think of?

3. What does this work remind you of?

4. Does the artwork address a significant human need? If so, what need?

5. Does the work relate to any aspect of your life? If so, what aspect, and how?

6. Did this work cause you to gain a new perspective in some way? If so, what way?

In addition to viewing art and applying group skills related to perception, interpretation, evaluation, and connection, older adults can also create artwork using these skills. Older adult creations can reflect personal perception of the world, unique interpretation of values, and the connection between emotions and artistic elements. This exploration assists in self-expression as well as communication during group memory training.

Summary

Thus far, I have presented three categories of psychosocial factors that affect older adult memory: social, emotional, and cognitive. This chapter has addressed how to optimize social factors; the previous chapter, Chapter 2, addressed how to optimize emotional factors; the next chapter, Chapter 4, will address how to optimize cognitive factors. All three of these factors are interdependent, and all three are critical aspects of effective memory training.

The following chapter describes the process of targeting cognition through art-making/art viewing. However, remembering the importance of all three aspects is essential before proceeding. Social and emotional well-being will ultimately promote cognitive well-being.

Chapter 4

COGNITIVE TRAINING THROUGH CREATIVE SELF-EXPRESSION

KEY CONCEPT: Creativity exercises the brain and provides benefits that parallel cognitive training.

WORDBANK
(Definitions can be found throughout the chapter.)

1	Limbic system	9	ATR-N
2	Cognitive reserve	10	Procedural memory
3	Visuospatial skills	11	Amnestic MCI
4	Inductive reasoning	12	Short-term memory
5	Episodic memory	13	Collages
6	Compensatory strategies	14	K/S, P/A, C/Sy
7	Restorative strategies	15	Working memory
8	ETC	16	Autonomous nervous system

Addressing cognitive abilities

Memory is very complex, and memory loss does not necessarily follow a predictable course (Helen and Padilla 2011). Over the years, I have heard creative professionals say that they aren't sure how much—if any—improvement in cognition can be expected. Cognitive functioning and memory can be targeted and even improved, but structure and clear-minded goals are needed to ensure measurable progress. Before focusing on cognitive training and memory enhancement, I will provide a brief overview of the concepts that are essential to cognitive success.

As mentioned in the last two chapters, creative self-expression can benefit the brain by enhancing mood and promoting dynamic socialization. Self-expression is emotional and enables mood elevation. When mood is enhanced, cognitive ability can improve, and depression, anxiety, and stress are alleviated (Chertkow *et al.* 2001; Fann, Uotomoto, and Katon 2001).

Additionally, as described in Chapter 3, non-verbal and creativity-based communication synthesizes emotions and thoughts in a way that is often difficult to achieve through logic and words alone. Concealing outward signs of emotion has been identified as a stressor that can diminish memory, communication, and problem-solving skills (Richards 2004). In contrast, self-expression through the communication of emotions can successfully alleviate cognitive impairment. Studies show that the emotional feedback provided in social settings can protect against dementia and AD (Chertkow *et al.* 2001).

Current literature shows that helping older adults to value their ideas, link life experiences to the creative process, and have confidence in their endeavors is a central component of the successful facilitation of creative self-expression (Brinkman 2010; Torrance 1965; Winner 2007). Creative self-expression is a very personal and meaningful process: internal thoughts, feelings, and memories are externalized through art.

Meaningful information is easier to remember and provides intrinsic motivation (Schunk 2007). An understanding of older adults' internal worlds is needed to continually set appropriate goals and to effectively engage older adults in meaningful creativity. Thus, the success of creativity-based memory training is dependent upon progress in the following areas, which must be prioritized (not necessarily in this order) by creative professionals working with older adults:

- confidence

- meaning-making

- enhanced mood

- culture

- interpersonal communication and collaboration.

Before reading on, please review these concepts so that you feel secure in prioritizing these aspects.

Emotion-focused interventions

In a meta-analysis of 96 studies, researchers found considerable overlap of risk factors for both cognitive and emotional disorders and determined that cognitive and emotional health should be addressed simultaneously (Hendrie *et al.* 2006). A study by Mateer, Sira, and O'Connell (2005) reviewed the literature concerning the impact of interventions (e.g. emotion-focused vs. cognitive) on clients with impaired cognition. The researchers determined that emotion-focused treatments may be more effective than cognitive interventions for clients with combined emotional distress and cognitive impairment—a highly common occurrence. The study revealed that emotion-focused treatments facilitate therapeutic conversations about participants' feelings on cognitive difficulties throughout the interventions and therefore enhance outcomes (Mateer *et al.* 2005).

Sessions focused on self-expression through creativity have the combined benefit of targeting emotion and cognition simultaneously. This, in combination with social environments, culminates in the optimal stimulation of the brain. As a result, creative professionals who apply the techniques outlined within this book are well positioned to target enhanced memory.

Targeting cognitive performance through creativity

The content within this book, and particularly within this chapter, aims to condense the lessons that I've learned from research and make them accessible to creative professionals from a range of backgrounds. Creative self-expression enhances cognitive functioning of older adults, and it is my belief that these techniques are best applied widely in order to benefit the largest number of older adults possible. Although cognitive training techniques will be outlined in later sections, creativity in and of itself is therapeutic and rehabilitative.

According to Perry (2008), an internationally recognized authority on brain development, creativity is rehabilitative because it involves experiences that are (a) relevant and appropriately matched to developmental needs, (b) pleasurable and therefore rewarding,

(c) rhythmic in the technical movements required and thus neurally stimulating, and (d) respectful toward people, their families, and cultures (Perry 2008). The following explains how these elements are incorporated into creativity-based memory training sessions.

- *Relevant:* Older adults use life experiences as inspiration for art-making, and allow the creative process to reflect neurological and autonomous nervous system functioning. This makes the created artwork relevant to the older adults' cultural and emotional needs.

- *Pleasurable:* By allowing older adults to stay aware of their breathing, heart-rate, and other automatic functions, they can use the art-making to relax, self-soothe, and engage comfortably in social settings.

- *Repetitive/rhythmic:* Creative professionals may apply their knowledge of the effect of art-making on the brain. Thus, they can carefully create opportunities that provide heightened, gratifying stimulation intermittent with opportunities for restful, soothing creativity centered on bodily pleasures. This will be described more in depth in a later section.

- *Respectful:* By considering culture and cognitive needs simultaneously, creative sessions allow older adults to feel valued. As a result, older adults may increasingly desire to share their personal stories and past experiences during reminiscence as a means to connect with others.

As long as a creative professional remembers these key aspects that are intrinsic to creativity-based memory training, such sessions can take on many forms. Creativity-based memory training can be provided during art therapy, counseling, or even arts for health and the format can be social/community-based or even clinical. One example of community-based, arts for health sessions were those offered as part of a multisite national study led at George Washington University by Gene Cohen (2006). His large-scale creativity and arts study used an experimental design to investigate the impact of cultural programs (e.g. painting, jewelry making, and pottery) on the general and mental health of persons aged 65 and over. With a sample of over 300 older adults, the study demonstrated that creative behavior enhances overall functioning, health, and quality of life among older adults (Cohen 2006).

Another example of a social format includes David Snowdon's 2001 work. Snowdon is a neurologist who is a widely cited researcher on the simple effect of lifestyle on cognitive functioning. Snowdon demonstrated that a positive outlook, continued mental stimulation, and social support are all essential in maintaining mental acuity. Snowdon concluded that "old age is not something to fear ... It can be a time of promise and renewal, of watching with a knowing eye, of accepting the lessons that life has taught and, if possible, passing them on to the generations that will follow (p.9)."

A more clinical approach to creativity-based memory training would include art therapy. Art therapy sessions include directives such as drawing and painting which have shown to positively affect cognitive skills as well as mood, communication, self-expression, and decision-making (Alders 2012; Harlan 1993; Kaplan 2000; Serrano *et al.* 2005; Silvia 2005). One study in particular was conducted by Rusted, Sheppard, and Waller (2006). The principal aim of this study was to test the premise that participation in art therapy groups would lead to positive changes in both mood and cognition. Measures of depression, mood, sociability, and physical involvement were evaluated and, throughout the study, participants created artwork with therapeutic connections to previous life experiences. As compared with activity groups, art therapy sessions produced longer lasting and more dramatic cognitive performance benefits and improvements in mood (Rusted *et al.* 2006).

Art therapy requires a background in mental health with a minimum of a master's degree. Higher education on the part of the creative professional may ultimately enhance outcomes and ensure standards of professional practice. However, a wide variety of creative professionals can and do work effectively with older adults. Regardless of educational background, it is essential for any creative professional to thoroughly understand the nature of cognitive impairment before targeting improved memory. Without this understanding, cognitive training through creativity will not be successfully executed.

Nature of cognitive impairment

Cognitive performance encompasses memory, concentration, and/ or coordination, and cognitive impairment involves deficits in these and other areas. The concept of cognitive impairment has evolved considerably over the past four decades. Petersen and Negash (2008) have summarized the progression of understanding in a review of the literature: the first attempt to conceptualize cognitive impairment dated back to 1962, when the term benign senescent forgetfulness began to be used; this was followed by the term age-associated memory impairment used by the National Institute of Mental Health in 1986 (Petersen and Negash 2008). Mild cognitive impairment (MCI) is a recent term used to describe symptoms of memory problems greater than normally expected with aging (Manly *et al.* 2008).

Classifications for MCI have since been developed, and one common classification distinguishes amnestic from non-amnestic forms of MCI. Amnestic MCI is characterized by memory impairment and often precedes AD; however, a diagnosis of MCI does not necessarily mean that a person will develop AD. In contrast, non-amnestic forms of MCI commonly relate to impairment in executive functioning, such as in Parkinson's disease (Petersen 2011). Within this book, the term cognitive impairment refers to amnestic MCI.

Although no single cause of amnestic MCI has been identified, there are consistent physiological changes associated with MCI, such as shrinkage of the hippocampus and abnormal clumps of beta-amyloid protein (i.e. plaques and tangles; Alzheimer's Association 2010a; Grady 2008). Language disturbance (e.g. difficulty with sentence formation), deterioration of visuospatial skills (e.g. disorientation and an inability to appropriately utilize fine/gross motor skills), and deficits in attention, perception, memory, and motor coordination are all associated with amnestic MCI. These aspects of amnestic MCI can be targeted during creativity-based memory training sessions.

Language disturbance

During mild cognitive impairment, an older adult may have difficulties with auditory comprehension as well as with sentence formation. Research (both quantitative and qualitative) with older adults suffering from cognitive impairment has demonstrated that older adults can successfully produce meaningful and expressive artwork even when language skills have declined, providing a means for communication which bypasses language deficits and may even offer a means for rehabilitation (Cummings *et al.* 2008; De Petrillo and Winner 2005; Mell, Howard, and Miller 2003).

Difficulty with language can be a highly frustrating experience for older adults. For this reason, older adults need to continuously experience acceptance and success, especially if they are struggling with communication. Art and creativity can keep the dialogue going even when the words are limited (Helen and Padilla 2011). Research linking art and the brain has tracked art-making throughout cognitive impairment, and studies have shown that, regardless of language difficulties, creative self-expression is not impeded (Mell *et al.* 2003).

Not only do language deficits not impede the creative process; in some instances, they can actually enhance it. One's ability to "turn off" semantic knowledge (the "inner voice") and rely completely on visual identification is believed to improve the ability to create art (Chamberlain 2007). This turning off of semantic knowledge is a skill, and an important one at that. Even trained artists are inhibited during art-making if they cannot "turn off" the verbal associations of what they are viewing (Chamberlain 2007). Sometimes such sets of verbal associations "blind" the artist to what they are actually seeing; in other words, verbal associations sometimes inhibit visuospatial abilities. Relying on visuospatial perceptions has been found to aid the ability to identify and later depict objects and scenes accurately (Chamberlain 2007).

Visuospatial skills

Visuospatial skills allow an older adult to perceive objects in relation to each other and to him or herself. Researchers Maurer and Prvulovic (2004) have demonstrated that artwork can provide insight into an older adult's level and type of visuospatial deficits. While viewing artwork, researchers and clinicians have described the ability to "see the world through the patients' eyes," which enables a better understanding of cognitive changes (Maurer and Prvulovic 2004).

The belief that art provides insight into the internal workings of another's mind is based upon centuries of intrigue. Several modern-day theorists have pointed out that art products act as a kind of symbol for the mind that created it (Epstein 2002). In research, visual depictions of internal worlds have reflected verbally described perceptions of the external world (Freedberg and Gallese 2007; Miller, Yener, and Akdal 2005). For this reason, works of art may offer useful information about the subjective nature of experience (Epstein 2002).

Visuospatial skills include figure–ground perception. The ability to separate the foreground from the background is a skill needed to depict scenes (e.g. landscape; see Figure 4.1) in art. This skill is also needed in daily living. Individuals with visuospatial problems look for an object in a drawer, around a room, or on a shelf and are unable to find the desired object even if it is in plain sight. They may lose things against background objects and realize that others find the very things they were looking for easily.

Figure 4.1 Foreground, middle-ground, and background

In addition to helping the brain recognize and organize visual and spatial information, visuospatial skills can include constructional praxis. This is a task which requires the ability to interact with and manipulate two- and three-dimensional space. Constructional praxis is a skill necessary for goal-oriented motor coordination such as during art-making and driving a car.

Motor coordination

Cognitive abilities enable older adults to accurately perceive and interact with the environment through fine and gross motor coordination (Elias and Wagster 2007). The impairment of motor skills is one indicator of cognitive decline that may lead to early detection (Kleiner-Fisman, Black, and Lang 2003; Musha *et al.* 2000).

Motor skills are engaged during art-making. During an intervention, individuals learn to use various art materials and control fine and gross motor coordination in order to produce specific visual results. Such exercises position art-making interventions as a dynamic, therapeutic opportunity.

Attention deficit

Art created by older adults can reveal patterns of cognitive impairment such as a decreased precision and attention to spatial relationships (Miller and Hou 2004). Art-making has the potential to increase attention capacity through integrated higher cortical thinking (e.g. planning and problem solving; Hass-Cohen and Carr 2008). A pilot study conducted by Rentz (2002) exemplified the benefits of art-making in a program called Memories in the Making®. This research study implemented art sessions at adult daycare and nursing home sites, where participants took part in weekly art programming, using paints to express themselves with colorful images on paper or fabric (Kinney and Rentz 2005; Rentz 2002). The results were compared to participation in more traditional adult day center activities (e.g. current events and crafts). According to a staff-developed observation tool that evaluated seven domains of wellness, individuals in expressive art programming demonstrated "more interest, sustained attention, pleasure, self-esteem, and normalcy" (Kinney and Rentz 2005, p.220).

Perception

The brain's ability to organize, identify, and interpret sensory information to represent and understand the environment is a skill known as perception. Some believe that all knowledge is ultimately based on perception, and numerous studies have shown art to be a reflection of the neurological function of perception (Mendez 2004; Rand 1971). Identifiable visuals, which appeal to perception, are a basic requirement in art (Rand 1971). Visual perception during art-making depends on cognitive skills and is reliant upon an individual's ability to visualize and maintain mental imagery, both of which are central to functional memory (Vanlierde and Wanet-Defalque 2005).

Studies have demonstrated improved perception among older adults following art-making sessions. In one such study conducted in 2008, the researchers Kim, Kim, Lee, and Chun sought to improve spatial perception, color recognition, shape recognition, size comparison of objects, induction of emotion, and socialization. The sessions included tasks such as drawing common objects, family members, or self-portraits from memory and/or observation, drawing figures after viewing pictures of houses or portraits, finding hidden or different figures in a drawing, drawing with a three-point perspective, and making objects out of clay. Results from psychological tests conducted before and after art therapy treatment showed improved scores in visual perception, cognition, and emotional functioning (Kim *et al.* 2008).

Memory

Memory is essential for independent-living skills such as staying focused and completing tasks (Horlings 2008; Whitbourne 2010). During art therapy, the use of colors, textures, and malleable materials stimulates areas of brain located within the limbic system (Hass-Cohen and Carr 2008). The limbic system is a set of structures associated with the hippocampus and emotional regulation (Stern 2009). By providing opportunities for emotional regulation and increased mental activity, artistic expression in a therapeutic environment may have the potential to improve memory (Alders 2012; Stewart 2004).

My doctorate study investigated whether art therapy could provide cognitive benefits such as improved memory. For the research, I included 91 older adults (aged 55 years and older) from countries of origin as diverse as Germany, Russia, Dominican Republic, Bolivia, Cuba, and Haiti in addition to participants of US-born, African-American, and Caucasian decent. Five art therapists, each in distinct cities throughout three US states, provided art therapy according to their particular training and expertise to the participants at facilities such as community centers, adult daycare, assisted living, and skilled nursing facilities. Data were collected from therapist notes and reports, attendance records, demographic questionnaires, pre-tests, and post-tests. Following ten weeks of art therapy, cognitive functioning and memory improved significantly among the experimental group as compared with the control group.

Type of memory impacted

Creative professionals may work with older adults who are seeking to prevent memory loss or who are already suffering from cognitive impairment. Therefore, an understanding of memory is crucial. Cognitive impairment often affects certain forms of memory while leaving other memory systems intact (Ball *et al.* 2002). For instance, short-term memory is affected differently than long-term memory. Using this information, creative professionals can take a strengths-based approach and structure the art-making sessions in order to stimulate and exercise memory systems in ways that enable the older adult to feel successful.

Short-term working memory vs. long-term memory

Memory deficits are often most noticeable in short-term working memory and long-term verbal episodic memory (i.e. memory directly related to information such as names, times, and places; Cowan 1999; Tulving 2002). In creative sessions, working memory is used to plan and carry out behavior such as cutting pieces of paper or drawing a house. An older adult must maintain in memory what they are drawing in order to complete the image. They must also incorporate memory of what they just finished doing in order to plan what to do next.

The primary differences between short- and long-term memory are duration and capacity. Long-term memory stores vast amounts of knowledge and records of prior events (Cowan 1999). Short-term memory can only hold a small amount of information in an active, readily available state for a short period of time; in many instances, this information can only be stored for a matter of seconds unless it is repeated and rehearsed (Cowan 1999).

Procedural vs. declarative

Long-term memory is composed of two types: implicit and explicit. Implicit memory is involuntary, unconscious, and linked to sensory experiences; also called procedural memory, it includes knowledge of how to perform certain tasks. Explicit memory (also known as declarative memory) involves conscious thought and recollection and is divided into two categories: episodic (e.g. recalling events) and semantic (e.g. recalling facts, a person's name, or the meaning of a word). Recent publications demonstrate that creating emotion-based artwork in therapy provides opportunities to reconnect implicit and declarative memories (Lusebrink 2010).

Declarative memory deficits are among the first experienced, while procedural memory is often preserved (Press *et al.* 2009). For instance, an older adult may be able to paint an ocean scene but may not be able to remember the name of the beach that they portrayed in the painting. Procedural memory is the most sustaining type of memory; it is an area of preserved cognitive capacity, which facilitates rehabilitation during art-making, and it has a slower rate of deterioration as compared with episodic and semantic memory (Cowan 1999). Procedural memory involves a combination of motor, perceptual, and cognitive skills that, through repetition and practice, evolve into memories that are processed automatically (Cowan 1999).

The process of creating art draws on procedural memory; older adults must physically remember how to apply paint or form a shape. Relying on strengths to engage procedural memory is crucial for ensuring optimal performance and a low stress experience during memory training (Logsdon, McCurry, and Teri 2007). Creative professionals may begin a series of sessions with a kinesthetic approach that draws on procedural knowledge such as the Rorschach blot directive described in Chapter 2. Later creative professionals can then begin to introduce directives that rely more on declarative memory, such as remembering which brush to use for a specific technique or creating scenes that require naming and describing.

Cognitive training

Creative professionals will benefit from understanding the nature of cognitive training and how it is currently used in research and practice. Researchers and theorists now believe that mental stimulation may increase an individual's cognitive reserve, allowing them to compensate for and overcome neural changes associated with cognitive decline (Butters *et al.* 2000; Hass-Cohen and Carr 2008).

Cognitive training (CT) is increasingly used with older adults in an effort to reduce growing rates of cognitive impairment (Sitzer *et al.* 2006). In a recent large-scale randomized control trial, results indicated that CT delayed cognitive and functional decline in older adults (Ball *et al.* 2002). Some research has even shown that CT improved cognitive abilities for up to five years following the initial training with up to 40 percent of individuals returning to normal cognitive functioning (Willis *et al.* 2006).

Despite considerable progress in research, CT programs still encounter difficulties: culturally diverse older adults are often excluded from CT because of factors such as language barriers and illiteracy. Consequently, recent CT research has emphasized the need for more "user-friendly" interventions (Gallagher-Thompson *et al.* 2003). Effective collaborations with diverse communities are needed so that interventions can be designed and implemented more effectively with diverse older adults (Gallagher-Thompson *et al.* 2003).

The incorporation of art-making can fulfill this need. Cognitive training strategies fall into two categories, restorative and compensatory, both of which are applicable to culturally diverse creative sessions. The following sections outline how creativity can parallel CT.

Restorative strategies

Restorative strategies provide non-specific cognitive stimulation and, in many studies, have demonstrated the greatest overall effect on cognitive function (Pittiglio 2000; Serrano *et al.* 2004; Sitzer *et al.* 2006). Reminiscence is a restorative strategy wherein older adults draw on memory while recalling and sharing stories about their life and their past (Butler 1980; Woods *et al.* 2009; Woolhiser-Stallings 2010; Yamagami *et al.* 2007). In reminiscence groups, participants are typically encouraged to talk about past events in a supportive environment with the assistance of multimedia memory aids (Pittiglio 2000; Woods *et al.* 2009). Older adults have exhibited significant cognitive improvement following guided reminiscence (Woods *et al.* 2009). In addition to being an effective part of regimented therapy, reminiscence is an activity that older adults may naturally practice during social, therapeutic, and recreational activities. Reminiscence therapy is one of the most popular psychosocial interventions with older adults, and is highly rated by staff and participants (Woods *et al.* 2009).

Restorative strategies incorporate multiple activities in novel ways such as through a variety of social, leisure, cognitive, and physical programs (Park *et al.* 2007). In a recent survey study, art therapists reported that when minority older adults depicted pictures of their country of origin, they were apt to engage in life review and reminiscence while also staying connected with their culture (Bermudez and ter Maat 2006). In a qualitative study by Woolhiser-Stallings (2010), art therapy interventions used collage as a medium for personal reminiscence, self-expression, and the recovery of dignity and control. The interventions involved completing a collage with pictures selected from a box of miscellaneous, precut magazine images and writing about each image. Participants were first directed to make a collage of things they liked and then to make a collage about themselves. Based on subjective observations, the researcher concluded that collage may facilitate reminiscence because it may be perceived as less threatening than other media or techniques that require drawing ability. Furthermore, sifting through and selecting pictures in a group setting can stimulate memories and encourage clients to tell their life stories (Woolhiser-Stallings 2010).

Compensatory strategies

Compensatory strategies teach new ways of working around cognitive deficits—for example, the use of mnemonic devices to remember forgotten words or phrases—and often parallel educational approaches (Sitzer *et al.* 2006). Compensatory interventions seek to enhance three areas of cognitive performance: memory (e.g. verbal episodic memory), reasoning (e.g. inductive reasoning), and speed of processing (e.g. visual search and identification; Sitzer *et al.* 2006). Selection of these targeted areas is based on the following: (a) the early decline (i.e., by the age of mid-sixties) of memory, reasoning, and speed of processing, (b) the association of these abilities with activities critical for independent living (e.g. taking medications, managing finances, shopping, telephone usage, household management, transportation, driving, and meal preparation), and (c) the demonstrated effectiveness of interventions on these areas (Jobe *et al.* 2001; Willis *et al.* 2006).

Ball *et al.* (2002) elaborated on CT approaches for each targeted area. For verbal episodic memory, participants were taught strategies for memory tasks (e.g. remembering new words) as well as tasks related to cognitive activities of everyday life (e.g. recalling a shopping list). For reasoning, older adults were taught strategies that focused on the ability to solve problems in a serial pattern (e.g. identifying the pattern in a letter or number series) or understanding everyday patterns (e.g. prescription drug dosing, travel schedules). Finally, for speed of processing, strategies focused on visual search skills and the ability to quickly identify and locate visual information (Ball *et al.* 2002).

Expressivity-based memory techniques

Traditional talk therapy, upon which cognitive training is based, emphasizes verbal communication and literacy; this may not be the ideal modality for ethnically diverse older adults who often have English as a second language, lower levels of education, and lower literacy rates (Mungas *et al.* 2009; Woolhiser-Stallings 2010). Art is a culturally imbued aspect of all societies (Anderson and Milbrandt 2005); therefore, a non-traditional cognitive training format based on creative self-expression may provide a culturally relevant therapeutic approach to working with ethnically diverse older adults (Link *et al.* 2006; Woolhiser-Stallings 2010).

Cognitive training targets key skills such as episodic memory for language deficiencies, inductive reasoning for attention deficits, and visual search and identification for problems with visuospatial skills. Therapeutic sessions focused on expressivity may naturally incorporate cognitive training strategies while also:

- focusing on strengths and health rather than pathology
- providing alternative ways to successfully interact and achieve
- educating about memory loss and rehabilitation
- encouraging reminiscence and meaning-making.

Table 4.1 outlines specific ways that creative self-expression may parallel compensatory strategies of cognitive training.

Table 4.1 Overview of parallels between CT and artistic creativity

Stimulated area	Cognitive training	Artistic self-expression
Visual search and identification	Locating visual information	PERCEPTION: Deciphering and choosing images that include visual self-references
Inductive reasoning	Solving problems in a serial pattern	INTERPRETATION: Deriving meaning from images through interpretation and meaning construction
Episodic memory	Remembering details of stories	CONNECTION: Discussing details of life experiences related to artwork portrayed in artwork

Visual search and identification

Locating visual information is a common aspect of CT and draws on perception. For example, a participant may be shown an object very briefly and then asked to find that object among several similar objects (Ueno *et al.* 2009; Willis *et al.* 2006). Identifiable visuals appeal to perception skills, and are a basic element of art. As older adults become familiar with materials and techniques in creative sessions, they learn to be increasingly comfortable with creating identifiable visuals. Learning, regardless of age, is enhanced through visualizations, and visual associations have been found to improve encoding and recall capacities necessary for memory; the ability to visualize has also been shown to improve the speed of information processing (Caine and Caine 2006; Van Gerven 2002; Willis *et al.* 2006).

Art-making. Creativity-based sessions incorporate fundamental perception skills that cultivate visual search and identification abilities in a practical and straightforward manner (Alders 2012). For example, participants may be asked to scan an artistic representation for objects that are recognizable and personally meaningful; or they may be instructed to create a collage by choosing images they can relate to, making unique visual connections between the images, and selecting complementary shapes or colors.

To expand upon this idea, during a collage-making session, an older adult would be selecting images that they find meaningful in some way. This involves interpretation of incoming stimuli (e.g. the collage images) and converting the information into subjectively meaningful experience (e.g. this image represents my childhood; Schunk 2007). The older adult may also visualize memories that arise in response to seeing the magazine images, drawing on implicit memory (Fuster 2003). This process reinforces skills central to functional memory (Vanlierde and Wanet-Defalque 2005).

Art viewing. Viewing works of art also incorporates the perceptual skill of visual search and identification. When looking at a painting, a sculpture, or any image, older adults may naturally be engaged in an effort to decipher the images and make sense of what they are seeing. The older adult may also scan the artwork for any visual self-references in an attempt to relate to the artist and identify patterns (Yevin 2006).

Inductive reasoning

The earliest declines in cognitive ability among older adults are usually associated with inductive reasoning (Singer *et al.* 2003). Inductive reasoning involves the cognitive process of making inferences based upon observed patterns. Such reasoning is associated with higher-order executive functioning and is considered to be an indicator of intelligence and fluid information processing (Boron *et al.* 2007). CT programs place emphasis upon inductive reasoning because it is a skill needed for daily living, problem solving, and learning (Boron *et al.* 2007; Van Gerven 2002). To train inductive reasoning in clinical sessions, older adults are asked to form conclusions based on incomplete or partial information (Sitzer *et al.* 2006). For example, an older adult may be asked to list the next item in a series of items or to anticipate what will happen next in a storyline (Boron *et al.* 2007).

Art-making. The same interpretation that is needed during inductive reasoning is present during art-making. When creating a work, older adults may actively assign meaning and symbolism to lines, colors, and shapes; they may think through or reason what would make sense for a particular depiction, thus utilizing inductive reasoning on an intricate level. Similarly, creativity is said to engage reasoning through a process of higher-order thinking and problem solving, both of which are linked to intelligence (Hass-Cohen and Carr 2008).

Art viewing. When viewing a work of art, an older adult may analyze individual and combined visual elements (e.g. lines, shapes, colors) in order to understand the complete image and what it represents. Similar to the process of creating art, viewing art may require that an older adult derives meaning from images through interpretation and meaning construction, thereby engaging inductive reasoning.

Verbal episodic memory

Episodic memory relates to both factual information (e.g. events, times, places, emotions) and autobiographical information and is therefore highly valued in society (Tulving 2002). Older adults with an intact episodic memory system are able to answer questions such as *Where are you right now? Where were you yesterday in the afternoon?* (Tulving 2002). Several brain areas, including the hippocampus, that are necessary for episodic encoding of verbal material are vulnerable to early damage as a result of cognitive impairment (Miller and O'Callaghan 2005). When evaluating cognitive performance and diagnosing AD, clinicians (e.g. doctors, psychiatrists, therapists) evaluate an older adult's episodic knowledge regarding people, places, times, and situations (Becker 2000). During CT, episodic memory is stimulated through reading, drills, and structured tasks (Sitzer *et al.* 2006).

Art-making. Connecting personal life events, experiences, and emotions to imagery is what makes the art-making process meaningful. This connection is also what allows verbal episodic memory to be exercised. Creative sessions provide older adults with the opportunity to construct emotionally laden symbolic imagery and enjoy a heightened awareness of autobiographical information by making that information visibly perceivable (Malchiodi 2006; Marder-Kamhi and Torres 2000; Torres and Marder-Kamhi 2000). In cognitive training, older adults are asked to remember details of stories; during art-making, older adults may be asked to represent details from their own life story, personalizing and intensifying the emotional experience associated with memory training.

Art viewing. Artwork makes sensory stimuli tangible and facilitates a process of communicating factual and autobiographical information (Campbell 1999). Art-viewing in a group setting allows for components of the artwork to be identified, named, and defined in terms of their placement and relationships (Hass-Cohen and Carr

2008; Rubin 2001). Thus, artwork discussed in a group context requires verbal episodic memory, a skill that is often targeted in CT.

Table 4.2 is an outline of examples of ways that multi-step, creative directives may serve as a form of cognitive training.

Table 4.2 Examples of art session content

	Session focus and content	
1.	Visual search and identification	Magazine cut-outs are scattered on a table. Older adults are asked to select images that represent something about their life. They are shown how to create a collage. They are then asked to write a story about the collage and to share their story with the group
2.	Inductive reasoning	Older adults are asked about their family. Using plastilene, older adults are guided through creating a representation of at least one of their family members. Older adults are encouraged to include as many details of their family members as possible. Older adults then show their figures to the group and discuss why they included the details that they did
3.	Verbal episodic memory	Older adults are given an image of a city scene. Older adults are asked to name and describe what is in the picture (e.g. cars, houses, stores) as well as any memories that come to mind (e.g. living in Havana, moving to Texas, living in an apartment and going to college). Older adults are given markers and asked to replicate their memory

In the Table 4.2 examples, older adults are asked to create a collage, sculpt a representation of a family member, and draw a time when they lived in a city. The collage may cultivate visual search and identification skills through an exercise of choice, interpretation, and meaning construction when creating a collage. Not only does the older adult have to search for images that appeal to them, but they also have to identify which images represent and relate to their life or a life event.

The family sculpture directive may cultivate inductive reasoning as older adults remember characteristics and then think through how to replicate those characteristics. In contrast, the drawing directive draws on verbal episodic memory. The older adults name what they see in the image and then recall a memory that is related to what they see. This relies on factual information as well as autobiographical information.

Neurobiology of creativity and expressivity

An abundance of research shows that the aging process is kinder to the creative, active, and flexible mind (Cohen 2006). The reason for this may lie in the novelty that creativity offers. Novelty is inherent in creativity; creativity is a repetitious process wherein the "world [is] mentally constructed in many different ways" (Schunk 2007, p.287).

The brain is very sensitive to new information; however, over time, repetitive stimulation becomes monotonous, and its effectiveness decreases (Diamond 2001). Studies have demonstrated that the brain's cortical thickness (i.e. the outermost layer of neural tissue, illustrated in Figure 4.2) is correlated with brain health and hippocampus activity, and can vary with stimulation; one such study found that cortical thickness was less affected by an 80-day exposure to mental stimulation than by a 30-day exposure (Diamond 2001). The brain grows accustomed to stimulation and that stimulation becomes less effective as a result.

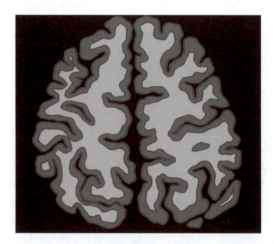

Figure 4.2 Cortical thickness

Through the combination and reorganization of previous experiences, creativity enables the mind to create novelty out of the mundane (Bracey and Dorn 2001). For this reason, creativity is associated with improved information processing and sustained levels of healthy cortical thickness (Chamorro-Premuzic and Furnham 2005; Furnham and Chamorropremuzic 2004; Jung *et al.* 2010). Research indicates that interventions promoting active social contact and creativity are more likely to positively affect health and well-being in the hippocampus (Greaves and Farbus 2006). By building on strengths and offering the power of choice and decisions, creative activity has been shown to reduce depression and isolation (Hannemann 2006). By perpetuating novelty, creative self-expression creates the opportunity for neuroplasticity, the increased production of neuronal connections in the hippocampus (discussed in Chapter 1) (Kempermann *et al.* 2002).

Theory: going beyond "recipes"

The content in this book follows a therapeutic, memory training framework rather than a learning or educational framework; however, memory and learning are closely associated and can be difficult to differentiate (Delahaye and Ehrich 2008). Learning is the acquisition of new information and changes the individual's knowledge or behavior (Delahaye and Ehrich 2008). Memory is the retention of that information (Delahaye and Ehrich 2008). As a result, learning is dependent upon memory, and memory cannot exist if learning fails to occur (Delahaye and Ehrich 2008).

During creative sessions, older adults will be learning to use art-making for memory training within a group setting. Cultural elements, such as collectivism or the emphasis of interdependence, affect the learning process (Triandis 2001). Research on collectivistic cultures suggests that group formats promote interest and motivation (Thoman *et al.* 2007). Additionally, individuals from collectivistic cultures may differ in learning style from individuals from individualistic cultures (e.g., immigrant Latino/Hispanics born abroad vs. US-born Caucasians; Gutierrez and Rogoff 2003). In general, older adults from collectivistic cultures learn most effectively through haptic learning, or "holding ideas in their hands" (Gutierrez and Rogoff 2003). Art-making provides innumerable opportunities for learning-through-doing, and as a form of therapeutic memory training, it may appeal to a collectivistic mindset. Comas-Dias (2006) described the differences in psychosocial needs by culture:

> whereas individualistic persons may require a mode of therapy that is verbal … collectivistic persons frequently require a therapeutic mode that values holism (using meditation, contemplation, imagery, and other connective states), acknowledges nonverbal and indirect communication … In particular, collectivistic clients require therapeutic techniques that honor and address the mind–body connection. (p.439)

Creative self-expression, such as through art-making, may appeal to a collectivistic mindset. Non-verbal and indirect communication is incorporated through the triadic schema described in Chapter 3. Additionally imagery and contemplation plays a continuous important role in creativity-based memory training. Many art therapists hold the perspective that the "healing power" of art comes through the process and creation of the artwork itself and there are many theories pertaining to how art-making enhances the mind–body connections (Hass-Cohen 2003; McNiff 1992). By combining art-making with discussions of the artwork, the needs of both collectivistic and individualistic cultures may be met.

Understanding cerebral activity in art-making

Noah Hass-Cohen and Vija Lusebrink are two art therapy experts whose theories provide a basis for addressing the cognitive performance of older adults through self-expression. Noah Hass-Cohen's (2003) theory, Art Therapy Relational Neuroscience Principles (ATR-N), is a system of six principles that provide art therapists with information on the neurobiology of emotion, cognition, and behavior so that they can fine-tune art-making interventions. ATR-N is based on findings that automatic responses of the autonomous nervous system (e.g. breathing and heart-rate) can be placed under conscious control during the art-making process, which can decrease stress and enhance mood (Hass-Cohen and Carr 2008). Through ATR-N, creative professionals can teach participants to synchronize bodily functions (e.g. breathing and eye movements) with art-making activities to enhance the therapeutic effect of the session (Hass-Cohen and Carr 2008). For example, an art therapist may direct a client to listen to music and create a scribble-drawing while breathing in rhythm to the beat. Synchronizing and maintaining awareness of bodily functions while creating art may help older adults to remain calm during increasingly higher levels of cognitive stimulation and memory training.

Another fundamental art therapy theory, developed by Vija Lusebrink, is the Expressive Therapies Continuum (ETC), which provides an understanding of cerebral activity during creative experiences and explains why older adults may benefit cognitively from art-making (Hinz 2009; Kagin and Lusebrink 1978). ETC is based on the idea that information is processed by the brain on three hierarchical levels of knowledge: (a) kinesthetic/sensory, (b) perceptual/affective, and (c) cognitive/symbolic. ETC offers a system of charting the characteristics of art products (e.g. graphic indicators) across the three hierarchical levels; ETC aims to assist participants in creating art with increasing levels of complexity, thereby stimulating corresponding brain structures and functions (Hinz 2009; Lusebrink 2004).

Examples of artwork and corresponding ETC

During my doctoral research, ETC provided insights regarding the older adult artwork which I will describe throughout the following sections. The Kinesthetic/Sensory (K/S) level of ETC, which represents simple motor expression and corresponding visual manifestations of energy and sensory involvement (Lusebrink 2010), can be noted in the artwork in Figure 4.3. In this work, the older adults focused on the sensations of colors and the physical process of placing the objects. The directives focused primarily on enhancing mood and promoting socialization (Alders 2012).

The Perceptual/Affective (P/A) level focuses on forms and includes figure–ground differentiation. The P/A level can be noted in the artwork in Figure 4.4. The older adults focused on planning details within the image, and selecting colors that were emotionally gratifying (Alders 2012).

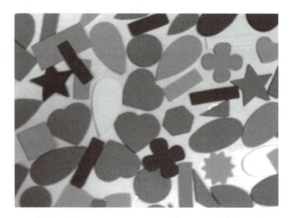

Figure 4.3 Kinesthetic/Sensory (K/S) level artwork

Figure 4.4 Perceptual/Affective (P/A) level artwork

The Cognitive/Symbolic (C/Sy) level emphasizes cognitive operations (e.g. illustrating autobiographical memories). During the study, participants utilized art-making to symbolize autobiographical memories and emotions. For instance, in the eighth week, the older adults at an adult daycare site in South Florida participated in a directive that included creating sculptures of their family members (Alders 2012). The older adult artwork from that session demonstrated intuitive problem-solving and symbolic relationships between forms (Alders 2012).

During this directive, several participants chose to create a sculpture of a family member who was still living in their country of origin, Cuba. Three or more group members expressed sadness about being unable to return home to Cuba because they "would be killed." One member began to cry about not having seen his sister for 50 years. This provoked one female member, who had remained quiet throughout the session, to create an origami boat without directive. She put her tiny figurine inside of the origami. Several group members, who shared the experience of immigrating to the US by boat, noticed her addition of the origami boat to the directive and expressed interest in making one themselves. She then taught the group how to make the paper boat. The group members put the sculptures of their family members in their paper boats, and some expressed a desire to set their boats to sail in the ocean back to Cuba. The group member who instructed the origami techniques informed the group members that the paper was strong enough for the boats to be put in water. Several group members stated emphatically that they would sail their boats to Cuba after the session (Alders 2012). Figure 4.5 contains images from the session.

Figure 4.5 Cognitive/Symbolic (C/Sy) level artwork

Both Lusebrink and Hass-Cohen suggest that art-making and its subsequent imagery provide a mind–body bridge (Hass-Cohen 2003; Lusebrink 1991; Lusebrink and McGuigan 1989). They theorize that when clients observe their art in paused intervals as it is being made, emotional and cognitive self-regulation are increased (Hass-Cohen

2003; Lusebrink 2004). Similarly, the authors explored how the human brain is capable of registering, monitoring, and representing its own functioning, especially during art-making (Hass-Cohen 2003; Lusebrink 2004). Together, their theories underscore the use of art-making to address cognitive performance in older adults. Table 4.3 aims to simplify how those theories serve memory training purposes.

Table 4.3 Theories that may guide creativity-based memory training

Theorist	Theory	Use for memory training	Tenet
Lusebrink	ETC	Using visual characteristics of art products to understand the hierarchical level of knowledge engaged during art-making	Systematically stimulate brain structures and functions; track levels of functioning
Hass-Cohen	ATR-N	Assisting older adults with placing automatic responses of the autonomous nervous system under conscious control	Fine-tune art-making interventions to enable synchronization of bodily functions

Educational vs. therapeutic frameworks

Both of the theories above, ETC and ATR-N, are therapeutic in nature. There is a reason why the theories I am presenting are therapeutic rather than educational. Although creative sessions may focus on older adults learning a tacit skill (i.e. art-making), the primary purpose is to provide dynamic mental stimulation and facilitate emotional expressivity in social settings. Older adults should be reminded of this regularly.

From an educational standpoint, learning content should scaffold higher and higher to levels of increasing difficulty. From a therapeutic standpoint, however, linear and increasing levels of difficulty can create stress and competition among the older adults, impeding their ability to enhance mood and socialization throughout the art process (see Figure 4.6). Such competition may impede older adult confidence.

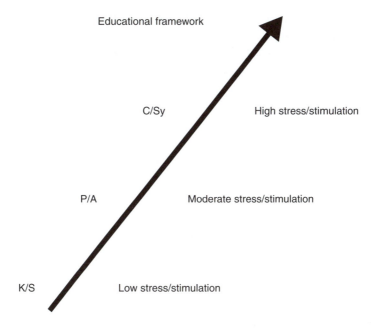

Figure 4.6 Linear model of increasing difficulty

Older adult confidence in their abilities is extremely important to their cognitive functioning. My past research repeatedly showed that educational models resulted in older adults reporting lower confidence in their cognitive abilities and memory. After a point, the more sessions that they attended, the worse they thought their memory was getting (see Figure 4.7). The linear model, which relies on educational frameworks and which emphasizes increasing difficulty, may confuse older adults in that they may believe that if their art products are not increasingly better then their memory is not improving. However, such judgements on the quality of the art are subjective and, for memory training purposes, unnecessary.

Figure 4.7 illustrates older adults who relied on educational frameworks and became critical of their own art. The older adults interpreted their own self-criticism to mean that their memory was not up to par. However, assessments showed that the older adults' memory performance was, in fact, improving. This contrast is concerning because older adult confidence in creative sessions can eventually affect actual memory performance (Alders 2011). Past research has found that those who perceived their memory as worsening showed poorer performance and had impaired memory functioning six years later (Valentijn *et al.* 2006). Self-perception is strongly associated with sustained cognitive performance in late-life (Seeman, Rodin, and Albert 1993). In memory training, it is equally important for objective and subjective memory performance to be improved.

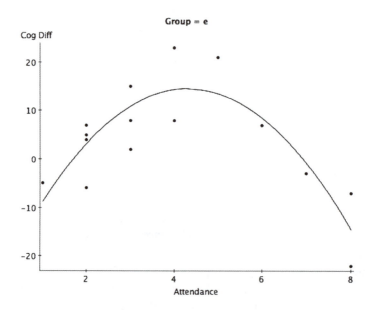

Figure 4.7 Self-report of memory

My research repeatedly demonstrated that the sixth session of a ten-session memory training series marked a peak in improved cognitive performance as well as a peak in self-perceived cognitive performance (Alders 2012). By organizing sessions with increasing levels of difficulty up to the sixth session and then tapering the difficulty after the sixth session, older adults are less likely to experience frustration with their own abilities.

After multiple weeks of cognitive training, older adults may feel mentally fatigued. As the weeks go on, this fatigue may turn into frustration and later be interpreted by the older adult as a decrease in memory functioning. By building up and then tapering down the stimulation, the older adults are able to continue engaging in memory training. However, the focus shifts from increasingly rigorous activity to progressive relaxation, improved mood, and socialization while simultaneously engaging creativity (Figure 4.8).

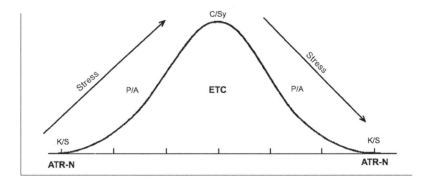

Figure 4.8 Therapeutic memory training framework

Structure and repetition are key elements in cognitive training (Willis *et al.* 2006). Such structure and repetition can be incorporated into creative sessions. Creative professionals can plan sessions which incorporate repeating cycles of increased and decreased stimulation to both engage and relax older adults. Older adults' cognitive performance benefits from rhythmic intervals of intense creative stimulation (C/Sy) interspersed with more soothing (P/A or K/S) stimulation. For example, a creative professional may find that a ten-week period of directives can be planned out in the following way to optimize cognitive stimulation while ensuring that older adults do not feel overwhelmed:

- week one and two: K/S level

- week three and four: P/A level

- week five and six: C/Sy level

- week seven and eight: P/A level

- week nine and ten: K/S level.

In contrast, if a creative professional were to hypothetically plan sessions with three weeks of K/S level, three weeks of P/A level, and four weeks of C/Sy level, there would be a linear and an increasing level of difficulty. In this case, a creative professional may find that at the end of the ten weeks, the older adults will report a lower self-perception of their memory abilities (Alders 2012). Mental fatigue may cause older adults to perform with less and less ease, and in turn, the older adult may notice that art-making requires greater and greater mental effort. In such situations, motivation may wane, and the stress caused may be counterproductive to cognitive performance.

Following a therapeutic memory training framework, a creative professional could schedule repeating cycles of rhythmic stimulation. For those creative professionals who work continuously, a sequence of ten-week durations of training could be planned. Over this duration, stimulation would wax and wane as in Figure 4.9.

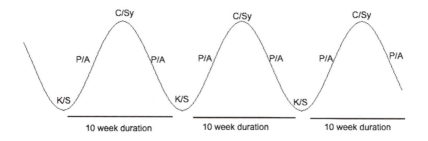

Figure 4.9 Optimal pattern of long-term stimulation

Summary

Cognitive impairment can come in many forms, and memory training can be a complex process for that reason. By understanding the nature of cognitive impairment, a creative professional can plan out structured sessions with a clear focus and goal. Cognitive training strategies offer a procedural approach to addressing memory and can be incorporated throughout creative sessions.

Theoretical orientations and knowledge of research help to guide decisions during creative sessions. That said, these concepts may be hard to put into practice without straightforward guidance. This chapter and the previous chapters have focused on "why" and "what" questions related to memory training through creative self-expression. So far, I have aimed to answer questions such as: Why would creativity improve memory? What should be targeted to improve memory? In contrast, Chapter 5 will address the "how" questions: How can sessions be planned to improve memory?

USING ART TO UNDERSTAND THE MIND

KEY CONCEPT: Structured art-making sessions may facilitate memory training.

WORDBANK
(Definitions can be found throughout the chapter.)

1	Session duration	9	Visual constructs exercise
2	Session frequency	10	Single directive sessions
3	Small group format	11	Stand-alone training directives
4	Predetermined session goals	12	Line painting
5	Tapered stimulation	13	Transformational image
6	Visual Conversation Activity	14	Information processing speed
7	Rhythmic intervals of stimulation	15	Opening
8	Scribble drawing	16	Closing

This chapter aims to offer straightforward guidance on how to plan successful sessions that benefit older adult cognitive functioning. Successful interventions entail many crucial components, including flexibility and knowledge of the older adults. Equally important for successful intervention is a non-verbal approach. Non-verbal interaction should reflect acceptance and respect to ensure success. Creative sessions should not place older adults in situations which may lead to failure due to inability or frustration. Instead, sessions should focus on three-fold goals: building older adult confidence and mood, enhancing older adult social interaction, and promoting exposure to an enriched, mentally stimulating environment through art-making.

Elements of successful sessions

Creative professionals may find that older adults require longer sessions; the standard duration for therapy is typically a 45- or 50-minute session. However, when working with older adults, this may prove to be insufficient, especially in group sessions. In groups, older adults may require session durations closer to 90 minutes (Alders 2012). As part of the normal aging process, some cognitive abilities decline with age; information-processing speed, learning rate, the ability to filter out irrelevant information through selective attention, and word-finding all slow (American Psychological Association 2010). Additionally, studies show that depression can lead to even more slowed functioning such as decreased executive ability, processing speed, and effortful attention (Gilley *et al.* 2004).

Many cognitive training sessions also incorporate this longer time frame of 90 minutes. Recent and landmark cognitive training studies have included 90-minute sessions (Ball *et al.* 2002; Tsai *et al.* 2008). Ten weeks of sessions, once a week for 90 minutes each, have consistently demonstrated to be a successful session frequency; this frequency has substantial increases in levels of cognitive performance (Ball *et al.* 2002).

In a review of 17 articles, the majority of studies on cognitive training used a small group format (e.g. less than 12 members; Sitzer *et al.* 2006). Small group settings are now considered an essential aspect of cognitive training formats (Ball *et al.* 2002). Therapeutic creativity-based memory training provided to a small group of older adults over a ten-week period may provide optimal mental, emotional, and social benefits.

In addition to lengthening sessions beyond 45 minutes (e.g. 90 minutes) and providing at least ten weeks of sessions to a small group, creative professionals may also find that deciding and announcing (e.g posting fliers of) therapeutic goals before beginning any sessions may promote regular attendance to sessions.

Predetermined session goals allow the older adult to know what to expect, understand the purpose of the sessions, and be able to anticipate upcoming sessions. This process may also aid in marketing the value of the creative sessions to administration beyond recreation, leisure, or arts-and-crafts. Table 5.1 outlines examples of a structured session, corresponding with clear therapeutic goals, appropriate session lengths, and formats (Alders 2012).

Table 5.1 Example session plans

Length	Directive	Goal	Format
90 min	Get to know your neighbor: Visual Conversation Activity (Liebmann 1986). In groups of two, select a colored marker. Without talking create an image. Respond in silence to your partner's drawing, adding images, designs, and visual elements. Afterwards, share and discuss the experience	Increase socialization, practice creative decision-making, visual search and identification, and inductive reasoning	Group

Table 5.1 is a structured session that allows older adults to get to know each other in non-threatening ways. Liebmann's (1986) Visual Conversation Activity is especially useful for this purpose. Older adults are able to focus on identifying what their partner is drawing in order to add to it. Additionally, the older adults must be sensitive to each other's interaction style in order to promote equal participation and socialization.

In addition to outlining the week-by-week session content, a creative professional may choose to outline how the 90 minutes of a given session will be structured. This may allow older adults to anticipate what's to come during sessions and ensure that older adult expectations match what is offered during sessions. Table 5.2 includes an example of a session timeline for a 90-minute session. The timeline includes an explanation of the cognitive training strategies that are incorporated. This timeline includes a directive related to collage-making.

Table 5.2 Timeline example for a session

Minutes	Target	Description
10 min	Verbal/episodic memory stimulation (short-term memory)	Set-up. Ask clients about life experiences since the last session. Ask clients what is remembered about the last session. Explain expectations and goals for the session
35 min	Visual search and identification	Collage-making. Clients find, select, and adhere images. Encourage clients to socialize, exercise motor skills, and accomplish multi-step tasks
10 min	Inductive reasoning	Collage completed. Older adults present and discuss one another's work. While viewing another's work, the older adult reasons through what is seen in order to make sense of the image
25 min	Verbal/episodic memory stimulation (long-term memory) and visual search and identification	Discussion. When describing personally created work, older adults are encouraged to identify individual images and reference those images to their life. Reminiscence and life review encouraged
10 min	Verbal/episodic memory stimulation (short-term memory)	Wrap-up. Older adults are reminded of the session's goals. Older adults are encouraged to describe how those goals were met. Descriptions of positive interactions, enhanced mood, and meaningful moments from the session. Next group foreshadowed

Additional planning for effective sessions

Chapter 4 described using a combination of ETC and ATR-N concepts, to enable structured creative sessions. Opening and closings to every session that fall under the Kinesthetic/Sensory (K/S) level can warm-up and cool-down older adult memory systems and decrease anxiety while creating social norms. Opening and closings are routine behaviors that all group members do to indicate the beginning and end of a session.

In Chapter 3, I described employing a schedule for each session to formalize each group process. An opening and closing could sandwich this schedule:

- OPENING

    1. Begin with a discussion or selection of a life event that will provide the inspiration for the session's art-making.

    2. Follow with a period of concentrated effort in art-making.

    3. Proceed with a display of the artwork created.

    4. End with a discussion of the group's art-making and experiences during the creative session.

- CLOSING

Openings and closings can establish a system of practices that promote interconnectivity and socialization. In a yoga session, the opening may be the "om" sound. The closing would be the namaste salutation. Churches often incorporate openings and closings too. For instance, members may stand and greet one another by shaking hands. At closing, they may gather and have coffee or snacks.

Openings and closings can help create standards for socially acceptable behavior. Non-verbal opening and closings are recommended as they avoid linguistic biases. Since culture affects how individuals communicate, openings and closings that are linked to basic motor activity may be best for work with diverse older adults.

Opening and closing activities should be rooted in the here-and-now experience and incorporate a process that is quick but that aims to enhance mood and heighten an older adult's awareness of their surroundings. Furthermore, opening and closings should be repeated every session to evoke a sense of predictability, enjoyment, and calm the mind and body.

The purpose of an opening and closing is to reinforce the availability of social supports. Repeated openings and closings also allow the creative professional to be on the look out for any signs of hierarchical inclusion which should be immediately redirected. During openings and closings, creative professionals can promote social bonds among all older adults within the group.

In Table 5.3, examples of openings and closings are outlined. However, professionals can chose to mix and match the varying openings and closings or to incorporate any that aren't on this list. The only requirement is that the opening and closing be related to an overt physical motion and that it aim to connect older adults to one another. Creative professionals would lead the opening and closing either through a verbalized directive or through modeling the behavior. As you will see from Table 5.3, openings and closings can be as simple as a greeting or more advanced like a mood rating.

Table 5.3 Examples of openings and closings

Opening	Closing
Each member takes a name out of a bowl. Names correspond with another member. Each member is responsible to hang the work of the member whose name they selected	Putting the artwork on display; hanging the work; shelving the work; achievements recognized
Check-in; participants use a Likert scale (no reading ability required). The scale shows five faces displaying five emotions; older adults color in the face with a selected color to indicate their mood	Check-out; participants use the same Likert scale to re-rate their mood (check for improved mood); increases confidence in self-knowledge; information can be shared with the group

Rhythmic structure and versatility in directives

Chapter 4 explained that older adults' cognitive performance benefits from rhythmic intervals of stimulation. A ten-week period of sessions was outlined to create a waxing and waning of cognitive stimulation while ensuring that older adults do not feel overwhelmed or burnt out by the end of the ten weeks (Alders 2012).

This schedule of increasing stimulation followed by a tapering prevents older adults from feeling overwhelmed. Providing opportunities for increasing and decreasing stimulation allows varied rigor. However, the older adults may ultimately self-guide to higher or lower levels of stimulation and creativity regardless of what the creative professional schedules and this is ideal. Creative self-expression can occur at any level of ETC (Lusebrink 2010). Although the creative professional may facilitate the focus of each session on a particular level (e.g. K/S) and emphasize the important aspect of the session during each week (e.g. here-and-now focus, bodily sensations), the older adults will ultimately decide what level of stimulation they will reach.

Any given level can be taken to a higher degree of difficulty by the older adult. For example, a K/S directive of scribbling colored lines while listening to music may appeal to an older adult's P/A level sense of design. For instance, a creative professional may prompt older adults in a K/S directive to: "Listen to the music and let the rhythm guide your hand as you draw lines over the page. Simply make lines." However, the older adult may want to incorporate or create patterns of forms using the shapes caused by the lines that crossed and met throughout the page. They may color in the forms and accentuate those forms thereby creating a composition based on design, space use, shapes, and more. They may talk about how the complementary forms and lines appeal to them. In this instance, the older adult would have taken a K/S directive to the P/A level and that is perfectly acceptable.

Likewise, a creative professional may show older adults a print of an artwork and ask: "Describe what [lines, colors, forms] you see in this image." This directive would provide P/A level stimulation. However, this directive may evoke involuntary memories to surface for the older adult. The older adult may remember a moment from their own childhood. When the older adult is ready to create their own work, the creative professional may prompt: "Based on the forms and lines that you saw in the image, create a work of art that is a response. Include forms, lines, colors, and more that you believe relate to the ones that you saw." However, the older adults may instead create artwork based on the memories that were brought to mind while viewing the work showed to them. This would take the directive to the C/Sy level. Conversely if an older adult chooses to simply create an agitated scribble in response to wanting to explore the texture of the pastels that they have never used before, the older adult would have taken the directive to a K/S level of stimulation and that is OK too. The older adult will choose to do what is most emotionally gratifying for them in the moment. As long as this enhances their mood and increases socialization, their response to the directive may be sufficiently stimulating.

Outline of ten weeks of sessions

By participating in all ten weeks, older adults have the opportunity to experience optimal training through creativity. Each of the weeks will target distinct functioning and understanding. Creative professionals who pre-plan and understand the targeted stimulation that they assign for each week will be better able to focus the directives and the group.

Week one and two: creative behavior during K/S

The Kinesthetic/Sensory (K/S) level of ETC represents simple motor expression and corresponds with visual manifestations that result from sensory exploration (Lusebrink 2010). During these two weeks, older adults will focus on the sensations of colors, the texture of the medium, and the process of forming lines and shapes. A creative professional may use these weeks to allow older adults to explore a new medium or technique; to feel the sensation of paint moving across the page with a variety of brushes for example (e.g. mop vs. fan brush).

K/S directives would focus primarily on mood enhancement and exercising cognitive skills through multi-step instructions centered on the here-and-now experience (Alders 2012). Older adults would be encouraged to relax and experiment with their movements. The resulting creation may often be abstract and so verbal episodic descriptions are needed during each session. After creating the work, the older adult could explain and name the colors, place shapes and form lines as well as any associations or sensory experiences that arose.

During the first two weeks, older adults could rely on procedural memory through a combination of motor, perceptual, and cognitive skills which allow older adults to make marks on the page or in the medium (Logsdon *et al.* 2007). Additionally, since the K/S puts an emphasis on the physical act of creating, these weeks will be directly related to the senses (e.g. touch, sight) and will facilitate incorporating ATR-N concepts. Older adults should be encouraged to be aware of their breathing, heart-rate, and temperature during the art-making.

Bodily pleasures will be the focus of the K/S level and these two weeks will allow the older adult to experience their body's physical sensations to the fullest. These sessions may result in older adults feeling "alive" possibly releasing serotonin and triggering alpha brain waves. Creative professionals should direct older adults to focus the tactile sensations (e.g. squishing paint between paper). During the K/S stage, the creative professional has the opportunity to help older adults feel calm, which may facilitate relaxed and appropriate social interaction.

Once the artwork is made, older adult mood may be heightened. After the creation of artwork, engaging an older adult's explicit memory (e.g. declarative memory) would further benefit their cognitive training. For instance, creative professionals may ask "What happened during the creative process? What sensations did you experience?" or "What is this color/line/shape called?"

Since the K/S level does not necessarily require any given artistic skill, beginning sessions at this level may provide a means for de-centering whereas professionals promote interest among members in one another. At this stage of creativity, older adults would not have the opportunity to compare artistic talent as a means to ostracize or exclude. Everyone is engaging in the moment and this creates a basis for positive interaction. In this way, the K/S level can initiate a social process that facilitates building rapport and communication and therefore assist in goals related to memory training (Talamantes *et al.* 2010).

In the K/S level, the creativity professional has the opportunity to establish the routine of social and expressive art-making, art viewing, and art discussions. Even if a creative professional chooses to demonstrate an art technique, the focus of the older adults should be on the feel of the moment, and the visual/sensory effect created. For example, you may direct an older adult to do the following: "Put water on the fan brush, dip the brush in paint, and then drag the brush across the page." Older adults may replicate; however, their focus should be on the physical act of dragging the brush across the page and on the feeling of the brush's bristles against the page. Older adults may name the techniques learned and exercise verbal/episodic memory.

The K/S level starts off with small, manageable creative directives and then progressively moves towards more complex tasks (Lusebrink 2010). Table 5.4 includes directives that may help an older adult to exercise the K/S level. Both directives have been referenced in previous sections and include the Rorschach blot and an exploration of the texture and effect of paint brushes.

**Table 5.4 Week one and two: Kinesthetic/
Sensory level (2 sessions/2 directives)**

Directive	Description
Rorschach blots; acrylic or tempera paint. Experimentation with color blending. Focus is on the sensations and the textures created	The older adult is directed to squirting a combination of colors on one side of a page and then folding the page in two. This creates an effect whereas an abstract pattern is duplicated on both sides of the page
Line painting with one or more brushes; acrylic or watercolor paint. Experimentation with texture and the feel of each brush	Multiple brushes are presented to the older adult (e.g. fan, mop, square, round) and the older adult is encouraged to create a series of line drawings by dragging paint across the page with each brush

The first directive example is to create Rorschach blots. In this directive, older adults may take pleasure in creating a combination of colors, carefully folding the paper, and seeing an abstract pattern duplicated on both sides of the page (see Figure 2.1 in Chapter 2). The process is simple, does not require extensive planning or skill but can be exciting. The created forms, color blends, and the color patterns that emerge may be unexpected and provide a pleasant visual impact.

The second directive example is to provide older adults with a variety of brushes (e.g. fan, mop, round, square) and to encourage older adults to make line paintings by dragging a brush or multiple brushes all across the page. Older adults can experiment with pressure and wrist movement thereby creating differences in line width and appearance. Intuition and spontaneity may guide the decision process and therefore fall in line with alpha brain states or here-and-now states.

Week three and four: creative thought during P/A

The Perceptual/Affective level of stimulation puts the focus of the session on the elements and forms visible in the artwork such as figure–ground differentiation. At this level the older adult decides on line and shape mixture, size variations, and other aesthetic judgements (Lusebrink 2010). The older adults would identify forms in the foreground, middle-ground, and background and plan the placement of forms in these areas in order to create a work of art.

In contrast to bodily here-and-now experience linked to the K/S level, the P/A features experiences and higher pleasures associated with past, present, and future experiences. The older adult may think through the placement of the visual elements. Through this process of thoughtfulness, positive ideas and associations may arise and which may be associated with beta brain waves and dopamine. During the P/A level, dopamine may motivate older adults to plan out creative color use; this requires cognitive strategies and problem-solving tactics. The P/A level, and resulting dopamine, may facilitate a heightened awareness of surroundings and an increase in awareness of sensory information (e.g. color, shape, texture).

The P/A level may be coupled with an increase in older adult energy-level, excitement, motivation, and achievement orientation. Older adults may become focused on planning the aspects of their work to the degree that their verbal communication decreases. During this level of stimulation, creative professionals can encourage older adults to explore their own preferences such as through encouraging older adults to "choose the colors that you like the best. Let your personal preferences guide your color choices!" The directive examples in Table 5.5 allow the older adults to include emotional reactions that are linked directly to the forms of the art.

Table 5.5 Week three and four: Perceptive/ Affective level (2 sessions/2 directives)

Directive & Materials	Description
Photo collage: theme of happiness or joy	Older adults are directed to make a collage of gratitude using images to represent experiences and aspects of life that they are grateful for. Afterwards, the older adults show their work and describe their images
Mandala; pastels on paper	Older adults select colors and create patterns of forms, shapes, lines, and space within a circle. Color choices affect the forms that emerge

In the first directive example, the older adult would be presented with pre-cut magazine images. The older adult would simply sift through the images and identify those that relate to their life in some way. The older adult would make compositional decisions regarding placement of the images. Colors, forms, shapes, and creative inferences would guide older adult decisions during the P/A level of stimulation.

The second directive example is for the older adults to create a mandala. This activity requires that the older adult select colors and create patterns using pastels (either oil or chalk) within a contained circular shape. Color choice and use will affect the quality and type of forms that emerge from the geometrical and organic shapes created. Older adults may make aesthetic judgements when deciding on color, forms, and shapes to incorporate.

Week five and six: creative self-expression for C/Sy

The Cognitive/Symbolic level emphasizes the incorporation of autobiographic memory, and symbolic associations (Lusebrink 2010). In order to create from memory, the older adult would have to use intuitive problem solving. The older adult would need to find a means for re-creating an internal image with external materials. This process can promote self-discovery and even spiritual associations in some cases.

At the C/Sy stage, the older adult will focus their energy on their own emotional state, and concept formations (Lusebrink 2010). The older adult would use their feelings as a guide for the creativity. Older adult experiences, thoughts, feelings, and memories would be conveyed through the artwork in line, shape, form, space, value, color, composition, and perspective. At the C/Sy level, the older adult will communicate complex ideas and emotions.

Being creative at this level can be deeply gratifying and older adults can become absorbed in the symbolic relationships between the forms. The symbols that may appear in the older adult's work may not be necessarily universal. Older adult history, culture, and personal circumstances will influence the image and may involve very personal interpretations and abstractions. Therefore group interpretations should be done only after the creator describes the image. As older adults may talk about the symbolic interpretations included in the images figurative language may be used. A creative professional should reference the attention back to the graphic illustration so that the group as a whole may understand the intended meaning of the description. At the C/Sy level, a deep understanding of an older adult's internal world can be gained as older adults share symbolic meanings and thoughts.

A creative professional's primary task during the C/Sy stage is to help the older adult maintain confidence and to promote a sense of belonging as older adults share idiosyncratic view points. Compassion is essential. Compassion is brought on by gamma states. Through encouraging compassionate interaction, the creative professional enhances the possibility of this brain state. Gamma brain waves promote acetylcholine release which is associated with innovation, memory, and sociability. The following two directives in Table 5.6 aim to encourage the sharing of personal, autobiographic experiences and may evoke higher levels of reasoning and symbolism.

Table 5.6 Week five and six: Cognitive/ Symbolic level (2 sessions/2 directives)

Directive	Description
Transformational image	Aging allows for life transformations to occur. Older adults are directed to create an image showing how they are transforming. Afterwards, they discuss the artwork
A childhood memory	Using materials of their choice, older adults recreate a childhood memory that contributed to who they are today

The first directive example asks that an older adult create an image which illustrates how they are personally growing/transforming. Late-life is full of change and that change can be interpreted as transformational (e.g. emotional, spiritual, physical). Not all older adults will be able to create on this symbolic level so an alternative directive may be to ask an older adult to select an animal or plant that they feel represents their primary characteristic/current life stage/manner of growth. Miniature figurines of animals or images of trees and flowers can be provided to older adults to help spark ideas. Creative professionals may also choose to reference real and mythical animals that transform or go through metamorphosis (butterfly, phoenix) and ask that the older adults select and represent themselves using this concept as inspiration.

In response to this directive, an older adult may choose to portray themselves as a rose and describe how they feel that aging is an elegant process but that it can be angering as well. The older adult may illustrate the rose as blooming in the winter and describe that they feel that they are aging too soon and describe a sense of longing in regards to everything they have yet to do. In contrast, another older adult may chose to represent themselves as a phoenix and explain that their current stage of life is liberating. They may see late-life as a spiritual journey that decreases limitations and provides a sense of wisdom.

The second directive example includes the prompt to create a childhood memory. To spark that memory, a creative professional may choose to present older adults with a box of found objects from which they can select an item to use as a source of inspiration. For instance, an older adult may select a feather and be reminded of a pet bird that they owned as a child. The older adult may then choose to re-create a specific memory of a time that they held and interacted with the bird.

Week seven and eight: Perceptive/Affective level revisited

During weeks seven and eight, older adults may once again be guided through the P/A level of stimulation in an attempt to taper the amount of structured stimulation. Older adults may choose to continue creating with higher symbolic and cognitive content but the focus of the session will once again be on the perceptual and affective information such as what they are seeing on the page (e.g. color, line) and their emotional reaction to individual visual elements. Older adults may be encouraged to ask themselves questions regarding the forms and composition such as, "Was this form my goal? Is this how I wanted the composition to look?"

These types of questions focus on the perceptual information and once again rely on decisions about the aesthetic variations. This information draws on short-term working memory: "What was it that I learned about creating hatching with a fan brush? How did hatching look again? Are these hatching lines that I am making?" Rather than requiring older adults to create highly symbolic content and simultaneously focus on the technical skills, the creative professional can give directives that feature emotions but that require a focus on line, form, shape, and other visual elements. Table 5.7 outlines two such directives.

Table 5.7 Week seven and eight: Perceptive/Affective level

Directive	Description
Rhyne's Visual Constructs exercise: quickly draw a reaction to an emotion as it is called out; pastels on paper; a separate sheet of paper for each of the 15 emotions	Older adults represent 15 separate emotions. The creative professional calls out emotions and the older adults use visual elements to represent them. Examples of emotions: excited, in love, angry, sad, guilty, joy, happiness
Create a response work to another piece of art; mixed media	Older adults are asked: "Where does this work lead your eyes? What/where is the focal point? What aspects are most noticeable?" Older adults then create a work of art in response

In the first directive example, older adults are read an emotion word and asked to create a representation of the lines, colors, and forms that they perceive are associated with that emotion. This directive is modeled after Rhyne's (1979) Visual Constructs Exercise. To keep the focus on the perceptual and affective qualities, older adults should be directed to draw how the emotion looks according to visual elements. Depictions of scenes and specific memories should be avoided in order to remain at the P/A level. Instead, if an older adult associates red, zigzag lines that move up and diagonally across the page as associated with anger, then that is the form that they should create.

The second directive example asks older adults to view a work of art and to visually locate aspects of the artwork such as the patterns of colors, placement of the lines, and any forms that are of interest to the older adult. Then the older adult is asked to create only those forms without viewing the original work. The older adult should be informed that they are not being instructed to recreate the image itself or to try to reproduce a replica. Instead, older adults are simply transferring perceptual content that they found most identifiable about the original work. For instance, if older adults are shown a landscape image of mountains and trees, one older adult may notice the color of the setting sun and the shape of the mountains. Their response may be to simply draw two inverted U shapes representing the mountain scape and broad brush stokes of swiped colors to represent the sunset. Another older adult who viewed the same work may have noticed a particular tree with many branches in front of the mountains along with the snow on top of the mountain. In their drawing they would emphasize these features. As a result, even if all older adults view the same image, each of their drawings will emphasize different observed visual elements.

Week nine and ten: Kinesthetic/Sensory level revisited

During weeks nine and ten, older adults may once again be guided through the K/S level of stimulation. Creative professionals can use these two weeks to refocus the group on positive interaction and to facilitate a positive final experience. The goal of these two weeks would be to decrease any stress that was observed and encourage an enhanced mood. In the final weeks, older adults should be asked to focus on their sensory experiences in order to concentrate on a state of calmness. Older adults should also be encouraged to increase interaction with the other members. The directives outlined in Table 5.8 may help older adults to achieve these goals.

Table 5.8 Week nine and ten: Kinesthetic/Symbolic level

Directive	Description
Quilt exercise; pre-cut pieces of fabric are provided (e.g. silk, velvet, corduroy)	Older adults create a quilt by contributing a square to the square of others. Older adults pick the fabric that has the texture that they like best
Music to image; scribble drawing; paper, oil pastels	Older adults create lines as a sensory response to the music. They use a single line to explore the entire surface area

The first directive example involves quilt-making and highlights an opportunity for older adults to interact with one another. The directive also focuses on the textural sensation of the fabric. For this reason, it falls in line with the K/S level of stimulation. The process of allowing older adults to select fabric that they identify as similar to their own characteristics will facilitate later discussion. An older adult may explain: "I selected the silk cloth with printed flowers because I consider myself very feminine and soft spoken. Silk is soft and feminine and the flowers remind me of my garden." This directive also enables older adults to create an artwork that requires cooperation and, therefore, socialization.

The second directive asks older adults to create an image in response to music. Older adults would explore their sensory experience of the music and use that experience to explore materials and textures. The older adult would use art-making as a process for creating visual representations of auditory stimulation. The older adult may engage in scribbling and dabbing to create textures and interact with the surface and material in novel ways.

This can be a calming but emotionally centered directive. Allowing older adults to create emotional but non-threatening work aims to increase opportunities for interpersonal trust and social support. At the end of the ten-week period, the older adults should be interacting with respectful compassion. This directive may aid in reinforcing compassionate interaction so that the ten weeks end with older adults focused on each other in positive ways.

A single directive for all ten weeks

The previous sections described a ten-week duration in which each level of the ETC was targeted through a different directive each week. This approach can be considered more clinical in nature since each week is self-contained and artistic skills are not the focus. By taking this approach, each week is a stand-alone session. This format may work well in private practice groups and in community-based locations (e.g. community centers, yoga centers, museums, galleries) where attendance may not be as consistent.

In locations where older adult attendance is more reliable, a single directive that spans all ten weeks may provide a more dramatic sense of accomplishment for the older adults. The emotional attachment that the older adults may form to a creation that took 30 minutes will be much different than the emotional attachment for a creation that took ten weeks.

Chapter 1 described a portrait painting process and that process is outlined in the following according to the ETC levels. Incorporating a single directive, such as a portrait painted with acrylic on canvas, may require a higher emphasis on creative techniques and learned creative behavior, but the focus can and should remain therapeutic. This single directive approach may appeal to creative professionals who may not have a mental health or clinical background, and creative professionals may find that graphic indicators relating to cognitive impairment may be more obvious in a single, progressive work. This should be addressed accordingly with referrals or consultations.

Week one (K/S) directive

"Bring in an enlarged, photo-copied picture of the grandchild. Single subject, close-up, head shots without many objects in the background are best. Using a ruler, draw vertical and horizontal lines, creating a measured grid on the image."

During this first week, the older adult would focus on the kinetic process of simply drawing the lines in a repetitive and methodical process. Motor action and movement should be the primary focus and the older adult's attention should be on the creation of straight lines in alignment. The creative professional should encourage frequent breaks from this process to promote socialization. The older adults may be directed to stand and walk around or to show each other their respective photos.

Week two (K/S) directive

"Put gesso on a stretched canvas. Once it dries, draw gridded lines over the canvas. Create a larger grid that replicates what you created on the photo-copy last week."

Gesso on canvas can provide a rich sensory experience. Gesso is white and so it may provide a low anxiety introduction to painting. The older adults should be directed to explore the texture of the gesso as it moves across the canvas. Creative professionals may choose to play relaxing music and encourage older adults to move in sync with the sounds, to be conscious of their breathing and to relax shoulder muscles while moving the whole arm to paint. This incorporates ATR-N concepts of synchronizing body functions with art-making, creating opportunities for a mind–body bridge experience. While the the gesso dries, creative professionals should once again encourage positive socialization.

Week three (P/A) directive

"View the grids over the photo-copy. Notice the forms, geometric and organic shapes and the straight, curved, and angled lines that are contained within each of the squares. Copy these elements from each grid on the photo onto the larger grid on the canvas."

Prior to drawing the visual elements, creative professionals should engage the older adults in a discussion of perception. A creative professional may ask older adults to verbally identify what shapes, forms, and lines they see in each grid before attempting to draw them. Drawing a loved one can be an emotional experience and any emotions that are brought up should be validated by the creative professional. This process will require older adults to correctly identify variations in visual elements and they may need guidance such as through modeling.

Week four (P/A) directive

"Put paint on all areas that contain cool colored shadows (e.g. low values of blue, green)."

This process will create a separation between the foreground and background. Cool colors are often found where two objects overlap or meet and where there is intricate detail (e.g. eye lashes, eyebrows, parts in hair). Putting cool colors will create dynamic outlines. Before beginning to paint, older adults should once again be led in a discussion regarding perception. A creative professional may ask older adults to verbally identify where cool colors are present on their image before applying paint. This will help older adults to be able to understand the descriptive use of color.

Week five (C/Sy) directive

"Put paint on all areas that contain warm colored shadows (e.g. low values of reds, violet)." Reminiscing may be the most effective start to this session. A creative professional may guide older adults in interpreting the expressions shown on the face of the subject (e.g. grandchild) within the image. Are they happy? Are they thinking? Did something make them laugh? What made them laugh? Warm colors are typically on the face around facial features (e.g. lips, corners of eyes, in the ears, on the cheeks, where hair casts a shadow on the face). Identifying these areas may require problem solving and may bring to mind memories. Older adults should be encouraged to take breaks from painting to discuss these memories. Guided breaks will be best to prevent any one older adult from dominating the sharing time.

Week six (C/Sy) directive

"Paint skin tones and mid to high value colors."

During this session, older adults should once again be encouraged to verbally interact before beginning to paint. Creative professionals should encourage older adults to make more symbolic and abstract connections between the image and their experiences. Older adults may use such descriptions as rosy cheeks, soft hair, and beautiful smile which elicit more meaningful evaluations of the picture they will use to create the portrait. When older adults break to engage in additional dialogue they should be encouraged to describe the joy related to their relationship and engage in self-discovery related to their role in the subject's (e.g. their grandchild's) life.

Week seven (P/A) directive

"Paint highlights with whites and yellows."

During this week, a tapering of stimulation will begin. Older adults will be encouraged to revert back to conversation regarding perception through such questions as: "Where do you see highlights? Where is the light source coming from in this image?" Older adults will rely on pattern recognition to differentiate locations that need subtle highlights. The highlights will allow older adults to accentuate forms and will require visual search and identification.

Week eight (P/A) directive

"Paint a color wash in the background. Pick complementary colors to blend together."

This session will provide a gratifying and emotional use of color, texture, and stroke. Older adults engage in an expressive use of color. The older adults can also apply a creative blending of color based on their personal preferences. Older adults can use discussion time to describe their perceptions of the blended color effect such as "The colors look like spring-time colors" or "The colors you blended make the painting seem like a dream."

Week nine (K/S) directive
"Paint the outer edges of the stretched canvas black; sign the work in the lower right corner."

During this session older adults can relax into a sense of accomplishment and focus on the simple motor process of painting the outer stretched edges of the canvas. Older adults can use daubing and blotting in addition to broad strokes. Creative professionals should encourage older adults to provide positive feedback to one another and describe what they like about each other's work.

Week ten (K/S) directive
"Varnish the painting."

The last session can be used to protect the work with a final coat of varnish. Varnish is clear and so the process of applying it is more sensory in nature, and so older adults can simply explore the texture and viscosity. Older adults should be directed to use long even strokes. Creative professionals may play music and encourage movement in rhythm with the songs. Older adults' discussions should focus on the relationships they've built with each other throughout the ten weeks, where they will hang the completed work, and what they have gained from the sessions overall.

Concluding the ten weeks

Following the ten weeks, the older adults will benefit from having their effort acknowledged. A public art show that invites family members is an ideal ending to the memory training sessions. If an art show is desirable, it should be planned from the beginning so that older adults have time to tell their family members numerous times. Ample time will also ensure that you have a chance to find an appropriate space to house the exhibit.

An art show will allow the creative professional, family members, and the older adult themselves to celebrate the accomplishments and achievements demonstrated by the older adults. An art show may also increase an older adult's feeling of confidence and therefore their desire for continued participation in future memory training sessions. You may find that providing opportunities for feelings of achievement will result in higher interest in creativity. Additionally, putting on an art show and inviting family to attend will allow older adults to further exercise verbal episodic memory skills as they describe to the family what they created and how they created it.

Having family involvement may provide an emotionally rewarding experience that will fuel optimal brain functioning and heightened motivation for communication on the part of the older adult. Through art, an older adult can reposition themselves as a center of attention. Other family members can show respect and admiration for the older adult, reminding the older adult of their value in the community and their family. Additionally, an art show will allow for you, as a creative professional, to highlight the value of creativity-based memory training. Once the art show concludes, art products created during the memory training can be taken home to share with family members, or additional art shows can be hosted in community centers to encourage continued social solidarity and interaction.

Summary

Creative professionals can provide stimulating interventions to diverse older adults and can position themselves as a resource to the community. Goal-oriented sessions can provide a means of ethical and high quality care, while structured and respective cognitive training through creativity can enhance older adult opportunities and access to mental stimulation. Through the creative process, older adults can form valuable emotional and social bonds, express themselves, and exercise diverse areas of cognitive functioning.

This chapter has featured information on how to provide sessions that meet the goals of memory training. Older adults can be guided through a clear and sequential process of ten weeks of stimulation. The next chapter will focus on where these services can be provided as well as what resources are available for supporting creative sessions.

Chapter 6

GOING BEYOND THE BOOK
Community Collaborations

KEY CONCEPT: Creative sessions can benefit older adults regardless of background and can be offered in numerous settings.

WORDBANK
(Definitions can be found throughout the chapter.)

1	Skilled nursing facility	9	AATA
2	Assisted living facility	10	SAH
3	Adult daycare	11	NCCA
4	Community centers	12	Intergenerational projects
5	Scope-of-practice	13	Clock Drawing Test
6	Graphic indicators	14	Webinars
7	IEATA	15	E-courses
8	VTS	16	Interactive/online galleries

The more creative professionals there are who offer creativity-based memory training, the more older adults there are receiving the benefits of such training. My goal is to promote an increase in creative professionals with this particular skill set. I have witnessed the positive impact that these strategies have on older adult lives and I believe that there should be a creative professional offering these services at every facility and center serving older adults. Any one field of creative professionals (e.g. art therapy, arts for health, creative counseling) may not have the man-power to accomplish this. For that reason, inter-field collaboration is important to effectively address the well-being of the rapidly growing older adult population within the US and abroad. However, older adults may present with complex emotional and psychosocial needs. Collaboration with a variety of professionals is the best way to meet all of the needs of each older adult.

Scope-of-practice

In today's competitive job market, professionals throughout diverse fields are increasingly focused on determining what they may legally, ethically, and professionally offer to the community. Expanding procedures, actions, and processes or scope-of-practice can enhance employment opportunities as well as benefit the community. As a result, scopes of practice consistently evolve to meet public demands.

Creative professionals' services such as in the fields of art therapy or arts in health may increasingly overlap with services provided by educators, counselors, recreational therapists, social workers, and psychologists, and this is likely to continue. The reverse is also true. Professionals in the fields of counseling, psychology, social work and more may also find that their practice increasingly overlaps with that of creative professionals.

Despite inevitable overlaps, there are many differences which distinguish one professional from another. For this reason, collaboration is essential. This book focuses on the concrete similarities between fields, namely working with older adults and focusing on emotional, social, and cognitive goals. However, whenever a professional finds that their interaction with an older adult would require practicing outside of an ethical and legal scope, referral and consultation is needed. For example, if an older adult presents to a creative session for memory training and exhibits signs of depression and anxiety, consultation with or referral to a mental health professional (i.e. art therapist, counselor) may be most appropriate. Likewise, if an older adult comes to a session expecting to learn increasingly difficult technical skills such as in an art class, consultation with or referral to an art educator may be most appropriate.

The creative self-expression sessions proposed within this book are not designed to be "art class" although there may be some confusion regarding this. The processes I describe aim to provide benefits to cognitive functioning. The emphasis is not on linear improvements in technical artistic skills even if those technical skills are taught. Instead, socialization and emotional expressivity paired with cognitive stimulation is the focus.

In my previous doctoral research, some of the older adults attended sessions such as arts and crafts and expected art therapy to be an art class. For someone viewing the session, who is not familiar with the therapeutic component (such as that described in this book), the arts and crafts session and a creativity-based memory training session may appear similar. However, there are many intrinsic differences. Not only is improved cognitive performance/memory a goal of creativity-based memory training but the relationship among the older adults differs as well. One therapist who participated in my research explained:

> the [arts and craft group] seemed to lose focus and structure throughout the study possibly due to the lack of group cohesiveness. [In the experimental group] when participants did not show for art therapy sessions, the group was concerned about where they were, if they would continue, etc. The control group barely seemed to notice anyone's absence. (Alders 2012, p.99)

Socialization is emphasized in creativity-based memory training. Socialization serves an important role. As previously described, not only does socialization provide dynamic stimulation but it can enhance an older adult's motivation to attend sessions consistently. Older adults may show friends and family the artwork that they created. This may increase discussions about life and social roles outside of the sessions, which in turn increases interest and motivation for continued involvement in the creative sessions/art therapy (Alders 2011; Thoman et al. 2007). The art objects provide a point of reference during socializing and allow the older adults to capture the attention of their loved ones and group members. Even if the older adult is living at home with a family member, the artwork may allow for unique interactions that differ from day-in-day-out routine conversations.

Cultural trends in seeking care

Older adults may come to sessions and exhibit signs of cognitive impairment. Addressing this is complex. Ethnically diverse older adults may perceive cognitive impairment in ways that are affected by their culture (Borrayo *et al.* 2007). For example, among Hispanic/Latino older adults, symptoms of cognitive impairment may be stigmatized as representing evidence of "sangre mala" or "bad blood," which would reflect poorly on family members who share the same blood line. For that reason, talking about memory loss may be more difficult with some groups than others. Introducing the artwork and keeping the focus on the art may be a way to bypass some of this cultural stigma (Alders 2012).

Research suggests that many ethnically diverse older adults share a collectivistic culture and prefer informal alternatives to therapy, such as community-based care and traditional folk healing approaches (Connell, Scott Roberts, and McLaughlin 2007; Wood and Alberta 2009). Creative sessions that aim to enhance memory would fall into this category of community-based care. Sessions that take place in public locations (e.g. museums, community centers) or even in homes fall into this category as well and such locations will be described later in this chapter. One of the reasons that diverse older adults may prefer community-based care is a general distrust of Western medical approaches.

Distrust of medical care

Distrust of the healthcare system is relatively high in the United States (Armstrong *et al.* 2006). Healthcare-related distrust may lead to poor health outcomes since such distrust often creates delays in seeking treatment (Armstrong *et al.* 2006; Berk and Schur 2001). Among some groups, mental health diagnoses are seen as potentially separating family members from one another and are therefore considered threatening in nature (Gallagher-Thompson *et al.* 2003). For instance, Asians often delay treatment/diagnosis by as long as eight or nine years after the onset of symptoms, significantly reducing their chances for cognitive rehabilitation (Alzheimer's Association 2010a; Mahoney *et al.* 2005; Minckler 2008).

Being prepared to make referrals and to collaborate with other professionals is important; however, understanding older adult preferences for care is equally important. When possible, community-based care should be prioritized when working with ethnically diverse older adults. That said, older adults will likely state who their preferred provider is, whether it is medical, holistic, or a combination. I suggest creating a referral sheet that includes traditional and non-traditional care providers (e.g. acupuncture, art therapists, medical doctors, educators, bereavement counselors). Forming relationships with a variety of providers is a sure way to practice with high integrity.

Caregivers

Older adults in late-life may find themselves living at home with family caregivers. Family members and particularly daughters and other female relatives often fulfill this role (Alzheimer's Association 2004). The frequency in which ethnic minorities care for their aging at home has been attributed to the patterns of distrust in the healthcare system, which research shows differ by race (Corbie-Smith, Thomas, and St. George 2002). Given the stress that often falls on family caregivers, involving family members in the creative self-expression sessions is a culturally competent approach. For this reason, home settings may be an especially relevant location for providing creativity-based memory training to older adults.

Living at home is more common among minority older adults than among white older adults. For instance, the percentage of Hispanic older persons living with relatives is almost twice that of white older adults; approximately 84 percent of Asians live with family members in old age; and approximately 62 percent of blacks live with family caregivers (Administration on Aging 2011; Aranda et al. 2003; Borrayo et al. 2007). The involvement of caregivers has shown to be an effective aspect of interventions for ethnically diverse older adults (Chow et al. 2010).

According to Talamantes et al. (2010), family caregivers may accept cognitive impairment as a normal sign of aging and manage severe, untreated symptoms within the family. Minority caregivers often endure high levels of stress and tolerate higher levels of impairment than is the case in Caucasian families (Alzheimer's Association 2004).

Long-term stress may even put minority caregivers at a higher risk for cognitive decline, enhancing the likelihood of generational cycles of cognitive impairment (Alzheimer's Association 2004; Rothman and Mattson 2010). However, recent research demonstrates that if culturally sensitive interventions were available, caregivers and older adults would be better able to address cognitive impairments earlier and therefore more effectively (Morano and Bravo 2002).

Aranda *et al.* (2003) demonstrated that caring for someone at home with a dementing illness may have debilitating consequences; caregivers exhibit increased rates of depression, physical illness, psychotropic medication use, social isolation, decreased quality of life, sleep problems, and decreased immune function. Morano and Bravo (2002) found that if culturally sensitive interventions were available, caregivers would be provided with the opportunity to gain an increased understanding, improve coping skills, and provide care to their older adult family members in ways that address cognitive impairments earlier and thus more effectively.

Sessions aimed at enhancing self-expression among older adults in family settings can provide them with much needed therapeutic interventions while also providing a means for caregiver stress reduction. An added benefit to providing creative sessions in an older adult's home or in a facility that enables family members to attend is the generational-leveling aspect of self-expression. Children may feel comfortable expressing themselves with the art media and may create an atmosphere of openness to the creative process. This may enable novel family interactions. Family members who are normally withdrawn may benefit from creativity. An intergenerational setting may foster a kindling of family unity that may be stressed as a result of the caregiving.

Inter-generational projects

For many ethnically diverse older adults, treatment for cognitive impairment is often provided either through increased family care at home or not at all (Gallagher-Thompson *et al.* 2003). Mental health diagnoses are seen as potentially separating family members from one another among minority groups and are therefore considered threatening in nature (Gallagher-Thompson *et al.* 2003).

The following topics listed in Table 6.1 have been found to be effective in expressive sessions when engaging both the older adult and their family caregiver (Alders 2012). These topics have been shown to promote social solidarity and have enhanced positive communication among diverse older adults (Alders 2012). These topics lend themselves well to family involvement and emphasize positivity so that the session serves the higher purpose of promoting enhanced mood and therefore optimal cognitive stimulation.

Table 6.1 Topics to engage the family

Group	Topic	Topic addresses
1	Unity	Inclusion and togetherness in the family and community
2	Home	Feelings of comfort in the environment
3	Family roles	Meaningful interaction that fulfills a purpose and social role
4	Community	Interpersonal trust and social resources for personal growth
5	Ancestry	Heritage and origins
6	Early life	Positive childhood memories that helped shape identity
7	Accomplishments	Major mile-stones in life
8	Romance	Positive experiences of deep and lasting love
9	Hope	Future goals and ambitions that bring joy to think about
10	Helping	Using wisdom to enhance the lives of others

Besides having topics that may appeal to the family as a whole, providing a directive that engages the entire family is equally important and valuable. Directives like those in Table 6.2 can lend themselves to both older adults' sessions and family sessions. For instance, the Visual Conversation Activity can be done between two older adults as mentioned previously or it can be done between an older adult and a family member/caregiver.

Table 6.2 Family inclusive directives

Family/caregiver inclusive directive	Goal
Visual Conversation Activity (Liebmann 1986). In groups of two, select a colored marker. Without talking create an image. Respond in silence to your partner's drawing. Discuss the experience	Increase socialization, practice creative decision-making
Name types of love, discuss experiences, meditate on a positive memory of love, draw the memory, write a letter to a loved one, or make a card with images	Verbal/episodic memory, managing emotions
Create an autobiographical timeline of your life. Draw a line and list years associated with important memories. Use collage images. What major life events have you experienced? Share in groups of two	Episodic memory, life review, socialization, visual search and identification

Services/systems of care across settings

Creativity-based memory training can take place almost anywhere, including older adult homes as referenced above. However, home-based sessions may not facilitate interactions with peer older adults, and locations outside of the home may foster new relationships with other older adults. Within this section, several types of community locations and facilities will be described: community centers, daycare centers, and skilled nursing/assisted living facilities, holistic centers, galleries, and museums. Each of these locations will be described in terms of their pros and cons.

Research suggests that many ethnically diverse older adults prefer community-based care such as a community center (Connell *et al.* 2007). As a result, adult daycare centers and community centers may host more ethnically diverse older adults than skilled nursing or assisted living facilities. Many diverse older adults may perceive "being placed in a nursing home" as a form of family abandonment and betrayal (Connell *et al.* 2007). Non-residential options are preferred among minority older adults, generally speaking.

Collaborating with community organizations like museums and galleries also has benefits. Besides providing a rich setting of stimulating art objects, gallery directives and museum directors can help to reach out to the community and promote memory training groups while also affording opportunities for consultation with other experts. Art museums and galleries are an environment outside the traditional clinical or caregiving settings and may be well received as a community-based care option.

Museums and galleries

Sessions in an art museum or gallery provide the older adult with different ways to engage in stimulating forms of creative thinking. Additionally, the older adults can be provided with many opportunities to explore aspects of themselves and self-expression through art-making and viewing. In a museum setting, questions such as those presented in Chapter 3 can become especially relevant (adapted from Anderson and Milbrandt 2005). Some of those questions are listed below as a refresher.

- What do you see?

- What title would you give this work if you were the artist?

- What do you think this work means?

- If you were inside the work, what would you be thinking and feeling?

- Does the artwork address a significant human need? If so, what need?

- Does the work relate to any aspect of your life? If so, what aspect and how?

The questions above exemplify how viewing artwork can spark insightful and stimulating dialogue among older adults in museum or gallery settings. Looking at a work of art and interpreting what is being illustrated and what is going on draws on inductive reasoning. Identifying the visual elements that lead to an interpretation requires visual search and identification. Furthermore, describing perspectives, emotional reactions, and thoughts regarding a work of art exercises verbal episodic memory.

Holistic and community centers

Holistic centers such as a yoga studio can also serve as a resource for community-based interventions. Offering a creative session in a yoga studio may provide the chance for attendees to experience a multimodal approach. For instance, in past sessions that I have given, yoga teachers offered to lead 30 minutes of "chair yoga" for the older adult prior to the art-making/ mandala group (see Figure 6.1; photographed at Dharma Studio in Coconut Grove, FL). Below is an example of a workshop directive which includes yoga in partnership with art-making:

Materials: White cardboard 10" rounds, pastels, markers, pencils.

Directive: Participate in a chair yoga directive (30 minutes); create a mandala after learning about the history of mandalas; create a mandala inspired by reflecting on a moment of joy in your life; after creating the image write a title for the work and 2–3 sentences describing what the image means. Describe the symbolic meaning that you assign to each color (optional).

Figure 6.1 Session in partnership with a yoga studio

An example of a response from one of the participants was the following:

Title: Atom-star-galaxy-universe.

Description: Four-armed swirl starting with white through the spectrum.

Colors: Each color of the spectrum.

Meaning: "Be here now."

This workshop is a good example of kinesthetic/sensory stimulation. The yoga session offered participants a means for relaxing and calming movement, while the art-making reinforced an awareness of here-and-now experiences. Breathing rate slowed, and participants relaxed into exploring the texture of the materials. Additionally, the art-making allowed for perceptual/affective (P/A) level stimulation as well. Participants planned out and distinguished forms and shapes. Additionally there was figure–ground differentiation.

Community centers are another location where art therapists may provide services. Such settings may provide a more casual and informal atmosphere for art therapists. However, a lot of advocacy may be needed at the community centers to maintain attendance (Alders 2012). Creative professionals may find that older adults attend community centers irregularly or experience transportation issues (Alders 2012).

Adult daycares vs. assisted living facilities

Adult daycare centers provide a protective setting that is less institutional than assisted living facilities. Adult daycares may offer creative professionals a structured atmosphere, with high attendance rates and a predictable start and stop time with minimal distractions or interruptions (Alders 2012). Centers such as this can offer weekly sessions with concrete and measurable goals. However, consent forms may be needed from guardians and payment for the sessions will require direct negotiation with center administrators and/or owners.

Assisted living facilities/skilled nursing homes also provided structured settings. However, older adults in these facilities will likely be functioning at a lower level and experiencing more severe cognitive impairments. In my previous research, attendance and measurable improvements were limited by the level of cognitive impairment experienced by the older adults (Alders 2012). However, at these sites, creative professionals (e.g. art therapists, recreational therapists) were employed in director/administrator positions, suggesting that funding and perceived capacities of creative professionals may be good (Alders 2012).

Offering sessions in a community center, a yoga studio, gallery, or museum can be a unique opportunity. However, getting older adults to the center will require marketing such as through e-blasts, fliers, and other means. Chambers of commerce often help to promote such

groups at no charge. An easier means of providing sessions is to offer
the groups in locations where older adults already find themselves.
However, regardless of where creative sessions are offered, there are
pros and cons to each location. Table 6.3 outlines the pros and cons
that have been discussed.

**Table 6.3 Facilities where creative
professionals work with older adults**

Type of Facility	Pro	Con
Adult daycare	Structured; non-institutional; high ratio of staff to older adults; higher family involvement	Older adults may not have guardianship of self, older adults vary in functioning
Community center	Informal setting; more opportunities for social relationships; higher functioning/independent older adults	Less structure, less funding, higher attrition based on transportation difficulties
Assisted living/ skilled nursing	Well-funded; director position opportunities for creative professionals; optional collaboration with recreational therapists	Lower functioning older adults, higher attrition based on health problems/death, older adults may not have guardianship of self
Gallery	Rich setting with interesting art objects that may spark conversation; gallery directors often offer a percentage of profit for any art sold as a result of groups	Less privacy; public spaces may lead to groups being interrupted by walk-in customers; marketing may be an issue; may charge for use of facilities
Museum	Large e-mail lists for marketing; possible grant funding to support programs; rich setting with stimulating art objects; optional collaboration with educators	Art-making may be compromised by conference room limitations; museums often have conference space but seating and space will vary
Holistic/ yoga centers	Opportunity to combine a workshop with movement activities such as chair yoga; studio may help to promote the groups	Marketing will be required; less stimulating environment; may charge for use of facilities

Getting started

Getting started with offering sessions to older adults can seem intimidating at first, especially if you have never worked with older adults. Understanding older adult needs is one of the most important aspects of offering therapeutic services. However, given the diversity among older adults, older adult needs are likely to be equally diverse. For that reason, collecting information on older adults before offering sessions may be important for understanding the older adult's background.

Understanding the needs of the older adult participants

Providing and collecting intake forms from older adults may allow you to evaluate whether creative self-expression sessions are right for addressing the cognitive, emotional, and social needs of the older adult. If an intake form is provided, creative professionals should be aware that older adults may need assistance filling out the form(s). The more information that a creative professional has on each older adult, the more culturally sensitive and understanding that professional can be from the onset of the sessions. The following is an example of a simple, non-clinical intake form.

INTAKE FORM

Name (Nombre) ....   Date (Fecha) ....

Age (Edad) ....   Gender (Sexo) ....

Country of Origin (Pais de Origen) ....

If you were born outside of the USA, how long have you lived in the USA? ....
(¿Si tu pais de origen no es Los Estados Unidos, por cuántos años ha vivido en Los Estados Unidos?)

Highest level of education completed: ....
(¿Cuántos años de la escuela cumplió usted?)

What was your previous occupation?: ....
(¿En que capacidad(es) ha trabajado?)

How often do you create art/crafts? Circle one:
(¿Con que frequencia crea arte/manualidades? Eliga una)

Very Often	Often	Sometimes	Rarely	Never
Muy a menudo	A menudo	De vez en cuando	Rara vez	Nunca

With whom do you live? Circle one:
(¿Con quien vive? Eliga una)

Alone	With family	In an assisted living facility/with other older adults
Con nadie	Con familia	En una casa geriátrica con otros adultos de mayor edad

Questions relating to education and occupation will inform the creative professional if this particular older adult may be targeted for later socio-economic discrimination by other members. Among diverse older adults, it is not uncommon for a third-grade education to be the highest level reached. Among diverse older adults, it is not uncommon for professional background to include such diverse fields as carpentry, cleaning services, and health services/medical doctors. I have found that older adults may segregate themselves by professional history in addition to educational background. This type of behavior should be redirected.

Furthermore, older adults may struggle to complete any given intake form alone. Their reading ability may be an issue; however, their eye-sight and fine or gross motor skills may also be an issue. If eye-sight or motor skills are a concern, one-to-one sessions may be a better format for that older adult. Additional questions that may be useful may include inquiring about depression, anxiety, or other emotional stressor. A more clinical and complete intake form can be found on the next two pages. This particular intake may be best used for determining if a group or one-to-one format is most appropriate for any given older adult. The group format proposed within this book works best with older adults who are only exhibiting issues such as: memory complaints, social isolation, depression, low self-esteem, etc. Any other clinical issues may be outside of the scope-of-practice described within this book. Additionally, if symptoms of clinical depression are present, a referral to a mental health professional is needed.

INTAKE FORM

Memory Training Through Creative Self-Expression

Services are for (circle one):   Self   Family member

Name of person to attend sessions: .... Age: ....

Date of birth: .... - .... - ....   Gender: Male   Female
       (month - day - year)

Ethnicity: ....   Predominate language spoken at home: ....

Relevant cultural or religious practices: (optional) ....

Contact person: .... Contact number: ....

Additional information: (optional)
....

Have you/the future attendee experienced any of the following? (circle those that apply)

(1) Difficulty with memory

(2) Depression

(3) Anxiety

(4) Health concerns/chronic illness

(5) Frequent misplacing of items

(6) Excessive worry

(7) Social isolation

(8) Shyness with people

(9) Difficulty recalling names

(10) Nightmares

(11) Recurrent dreams

(12) Difficulty verbalizing emotions

(13) Speech difficulties

(14) Recent stressors

(15) Development/personal growth concerns

(16) Vision difficulties

(17) Frequent frustration

(18) Recurrent conflicts with others

(19) Difficulty making decisions

(20) Guardianship concerns

(21) Parent–child relationship problem

(22) Sibling relationship problem

(23) Difficulty with fine/gross motor skills

(24) Change in living location

(25) Repetitive thoughts/behaviors

(26) Other ....

Explain: (optional)
....

Presenting problem: please describe the reason(s)/goal(s) for requesting services. (Be specific, if possible. When did it start? How does it affect you/their life?):
....

Estimate the severity of above problem (circle):
Mild—Moderate—Severe

Explain:(optional)
....

What goals do you have for the sessions? What do you/the attendee want to gain from the sessions?

Put a check beside specific goals:

☐ Memory training

☐ Stress reduction

☐ Increased expressivity (non-verbal and verbal)

☐ Improved self-esteem and self-worth

☐ Identity and relationship exploration

☐ Frustration tolerance/anger management

☐ Reminiscence

☐ Relaxation and anxiety reduction

☐ Enhanced fine/gross motor coordination and visuospatial skills

☐ Increased socialization

☐ Enhanced concentration/focus

☐ Decision-making skills

☐ Enhanced verbal communication skills

Identifying symptoms cross-culturally

In order to improve memory, professionals (e.g. doctors, therapists) are tasked with evaluating and managing stressors affecting cognitive functioning, as well as tracking and attempting to prevent further cognitive decline. However, this is made especially difficult with diverse older adults. Their higher levels of distrust delay the likelihood for early intervention. Additionally, traditional healthcare screening instruments that are used to evaluate cognition are vulnerable to linguistic, cultural, and educational biases (Lopez and Weisman 2004).

Given the distrust of the healthcare system among older adults, creative professionals in community settings will potentially play an important role in diverse older adults' lives. Cognitive impairment is more successfully treated when identified early (Alzheimer's Association 2004). Signs of cognitive impairment, such as motor neglect, perseveration, and disinhibition, may be noted as artwork through graphic indicators or the visual elements of the artwork; such graphic indicators may provide early detection of changes in cognitive abilities (Kleiner-Fisman *et al.* 2003; Musha *et al.* 2000). Art-based assessments have been deemed highly effective for clients with low education levels and illiteracy or with limited verbal capabilities (Maurer and Prvulovic 2004).

Creative professionals with a clinical background (e.g. art therapists) may be well advised to assess participant cognitive functioning before establishing sessions in order to understand older adult needs. Some older adults may have poor eye-sight or hearing and struggle to engage in group sessions. Others may have more severe cognitive impairment than others and may struggle to stay attentive. In such cases, one-to-one art therapy may be more appropriate than group formats (Alders 2012). Deciding on the appropriate format for therapy is important for older adult progress. Older adults placed in group formats should have the physical, mental, and emotional faculties to be able to benefit from the social interaction. Otherwise, a group format may create an additional stressor for the older adult and should be avoided. For instance, I have witnessed older adults single out others who have more severe impairment, labeling them "crazy" and ostracizing them. This older adult is not able to defend themselves and may not be able to inform the creative professional that such discrimination is occuring. This should not be allowed to occur. Evaluating older adult levels of functioning before groups are formed is important.

Clock Drawing Test

There are many ways to assess cognitive functioning quickly and regardless of the older adult's culture. For instance, art-based assessments and drawing tasks that can be used to evaluate older adult cognitive performance. Cognitive deficits affect artistic ability and can assist in early detection of changes in cognitive abilities (Kleiner-Fisman *et al.* 2003). Visual art-making is an expression of neurological function and can demonstrate how the brain organizes and interprets incoming information (Serrano *et al.* 2005).

The Clock Drawing Test (CDT) is an art-based neurological assessment that represents an objective measure of cognitive performance; it has been used by neurologists for decades to study changes in cognitive functioning. As a result of ease of use, the CDT lends itself to many different fields, and can be administered by a range of professionals. The CDT is non-threatening, and culturally neutral and also fits in well during creative sessions aimed to improve memory (Alders 2012).

The CDT requires an individual to draw a clock at a specific time (e.g. 11:10). One study conducted by Samton *et al.* (2005) compared the CDT to the Mini Mental Status Exam (MMSE), the most widely used objective cognitive screening test. The results indicated that the two tests measured different aspects of cognitive impairment. A retrospective review of records performed by Samton *et al.* suggested that the CDT may be more effective than other commonly used evaluations (i.e. the Mini Mental Status Exam) when assessing an older adult's ability to live independently. The authors concluded that the CDT may be a quick and effective way to assess cognitive functioning and is perhaps superior to MMSE in predicting an older adult's ability to live independently (Samton *et al.* 2005).

There is a strong correlation between CDT scores and brain health. Higher levels of brain atrophy are associated with a lower CDT score and lower levels of atrophy are associated with a higher CDT score (Samton *et al.* 2005). Figure 6.2 illustrates this difference in Clock Drawing Tests. The brain on the left is healthy and corresponds with a CDT score of 10. The brain on the right is experiencing severe cognitive impairment and corresponds with a CDT score of 2.

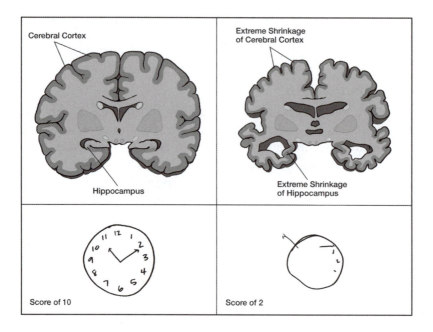

Figure 6.2 Brain atrophy and CDT score

My research has used the CDT to evaluate changes in cognitive performance before and after ten weeks of art therapy. The CDT scores were significantly higher among those who attended the sessions as compared with those who did not. Figures 6.2, 6.3, and 6.4 are examples of the CDTs from selected participants who showed notable improvements. These clocks were chosen based on the clarity of improvement, irrespective of ethnicity or location; however, all of the examples below are from non-Caucasian older adults (i.e. Latino and black older adults).

Clock Drawing Tests may be administered by clinical/creative professionals before and after a series of creative sessions to evaluate cognitive performance and any changes that may have resulted. Scoring for the CDT can take on many forms. I prefer the scoring method developed by Sunderland *et al.* (1989) because it rates on a ten-point scale rather than a five-point scale and is therefore considered to be a more sensitive measure of cognitive performance change (Sunderland *et al.* 1989).

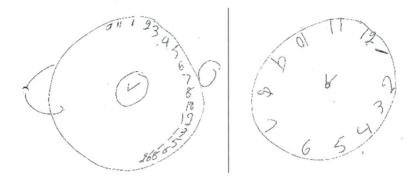

Figure 6.3 "M": pre-test score: 4 out of 10; post-test: 5 out of 10

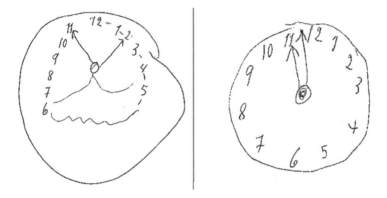

Figure 6.4 "R": pre-test score: 4.3 out of 10; post-test: 7.3 out of 10

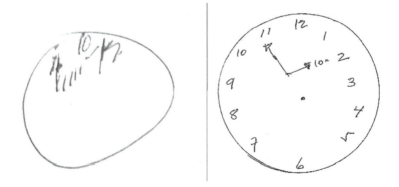

Figure 6.5 "J": pre-test score: 1.7 out of 10; post-test: 7.7 out of 10

Graphic indicators linked to cognitive impairment

Graphic indicators are observable visual elements that may reveal signs of impairment. In the previous figures, unnatural characteristics of the clocks can be noted. For instance, in Figure 6.3, the pre-test clock shows numbers only on one side of the clock. In Figure 6.4, perseveration or the same type of line can be seen in the pre-test. There are four hands drawn on the clock and the bottom two lines don't have an apparent purpose. This same repetition of lines can be noted in the pre-test of Figure 6.5; however, there is an obvious distortion and the numbers are not in the appropriate location. Additionally, the numbers are all crowded at the top. Below is an outline of the graphic indicators that are linked to cognitive impairment. For visual references, see Figure 6.6. Although the CDT may demonstrate these indicators in a straightforward manner, graphic indicators can be noted in any drawing or image. Indication of severe cognitive impairment may be best handled with a referral to a mental health professional including a medical doctor.

Some examples of graphic indicators that may suggest advanced cognitive impairment include (Alders 2012; Eknoyan 2012):

- spatial deficits/visual crowding on one part of the page or section of the drawing

- distortions or obviously missing elements (e.g. missing a number in a number sequence)

- inadequate or unbalanced use of space

- stimulus-bound responses (e.g. takes verbal directions so literally that completes the task incorrectly)

- monochromatic—lack of color use (only if color use was offered)

- objects on same page that appear disconnected/no relationship/greatly different sizes

- shaky lines

- conceptual difficulties (e.g. drawing a circle for the clock and then drawing a smily face rather than the time)

- objects that appear to drift off the page

- perseveration—the same type of line is seen in a constant repetitious use

- poor closures—an inability to make complete geometric shapes or connect or meet lines

- small images.

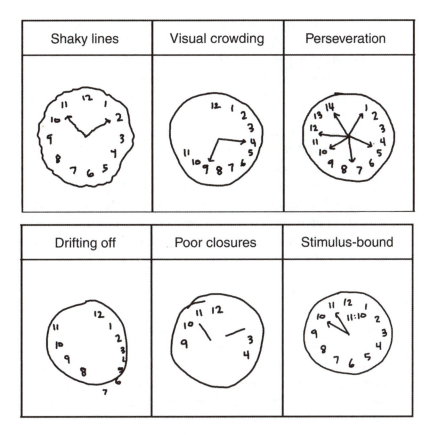

Figure 6.6 Graphic indicators of impairment

Understanding older adult self-perceived memory functioning

In addition to intake forms, intake evaluations may provide a creative professional with insight regarding older adults' needs. As mentioned earlier, the Clock Drawing Test may be useful. However, understanding older adult self-perceptions is equally important.

Older adults' self-esteem and confidence can affect their participation in a group setting.

The Cognitive Failures Questionnaire (CFQ) is a recommended evaluation for gaining insight regarding older adult self-perceived cognitive functioning. The CFQ measures everyday deficits in attention, perception, memory, and motor coordination (CFQ— Internal validity: 0.91; test-retest reliability rate: 0.82). The CFQ is a 25-question test. Higher scores indicate higher levels of reported cognitive problems.

Because the CFQ is a self-report, it is therefore susceptible to misreporting; however, research has demonstrated that the CFQ effectively indicates self-perceived cognitive functioning, and high scores on the CFQ are considered to be an indicator of increased vulnerability to stress (Wagle, Berrios, and Ho 1999). Additionally, CFQ scores correlate with measures of depression (i.e. Beck Depression Inventory) and with assessments of psychological well-being (i.e. General Health Questionnaire); low CFQ scores that do not correspond with low objective cognitive performance scores may indicate depression or a risk for developing depression or social withdrawal (Wagle *et al.* 1999). This questionnaire can be found online: www.yorku.ca/rokada/psyctest/cogfail.doc

Organizations

Creative professionals may be art therapists, artists-in-residence, recreational therapists, activity therapists, counselors, social workers, and more. Creative professionals may be hired by one location as an activities director or in another location as a clinical team member. Likewise, a creative professional may work as an independent contractor or in private practice and offer services at an hourly fee to a multitude of centers and facilities. For this reason, creative professionals may work in many different settings alone or with others who may or may not share a creativity-based training.

One risk that creative professionals face is practicing in isolation. Using creativity for therapeutic goals when working with older adults is a highly specialized practice. Finding like-minded professionals may be a challenge without knowledge of where to find support. There are innumerable resources, facilities, and organizations that will champion your efforts with older adults.

As the older adult population continues to grow, so too will the number of organizations, and particularly 501c3 charitable non-profit organizations that connect professionals to resources. The American Art Therapy Association (AATA), the Society for Arts in Healthcare (SAH), the National Center for Creative Aging (NCCA), the International Expressive Arts Therapy Association (IEATA), and the Visual Thinking Strategies (VTS) are just a few. Table 6.4 outlines these organizations and what they offer.

Table 6.4 Organizational resources

Source	Resource	Description
American Art Therapy Association (AATA)	www.arttherapy.org	Connects the public with the important work of art therapists around the world
Society for Arts in Healthcare (SAH)	www.thesah.org	Dedicated to advancing arts as integral to healthcare
National Center for Creative Aging (NCCA)	www.creativeaging.org	Dedicated to fostering an understanding of the relationship between creative expression and healthy aging
International Expressive Arts Therapy Association (IEATA)	www.ieata.org	Supports the use of multimodal expressive arts processes
Visual Thinking Strategies (VTS)	www.vtshome.org	Teaches strategies for engaging others in finding meaning in imagery. Involves skills including identification (naming what one sees) and complex interpretation on contextual, metaphoric levels

Each organization provides a unique perspective on methods and strategies. For instance, the Visual Thinking Strategies (VTS) outlines techniques for engaging individuals in a process of finding meaning in visual imagery. VTS would be a wonderful resource to consult when offering sessions in a museum or gallery settings.

The National Center for Creative Aging has a list of webinars and training opportunities for engaging older adults in creative self-expression. Likewise, the American Art Therapy Association offers a myriad of resources. One such resource includes a concrete list of supplies needed when beginning to offer creative services at senior living communities. That particular resource can be found at: www.arttherapy.org/ALFAToolkit/alfatoolkit.pdf

The following list has been taken from that link and links essential yet inexpensive art materials:

- crayons
- charcoal pencils
- oil pastels
- adhesives, glues
- tape, masking tape, painters' tape
- application tools (paintbrushes, sponges, cotton swabs, stamps, etc.)
- pens, markers
- gel pencils
- acrylic paints
- watercolor, tempera
- water containers
- sand clay or putty
- paper 8" x 10", 11" x 14"
- mural paper (tissue paper, cloth, origami paper, construction paper, etc.)
- magazines, newspaper
- miscellaneous items (seeds, beads, leaves, string, buttons, pipe cleaners, etc.)
- cleaning supplies (for hands, tables, etc.).

Ways to continue learning

It is hoped that this book has provided you with an idea of how older adult cognitive functioning can be targeted for improvement through creative self-expression. Reading this book one time may not provide a complete comprehension of the theories and techniques. For that reason, I suggest that creative professionals continue learning through webinars, e-courses, and test their knowledge with the following quizzes. These quizzes can be found online at: www.arttherapyconsulting.com

I will provide additional learning opportunities throughout the year via webinars (i.e. a short training workshop) and e-courses (i.e. content-focused online class). These opportunities will be announced on my website: www.arttherapyconsulting.com. Webinars and e-courses will be offered in the fall and summer or by appointment. I also offer in-person workshops to groups of professionals on a rotating basis or by demand.

For those creative professionals already working with older adults, I will launch an interactive online gallery in August 2014. What this means is that on my website, I will host images of older adult artwork (a photo release/consent is needed and can be on my website). The interactive online gallery aims to make it easier for an older adult's family members and the wider community to see and provide positive feedback and support to older adults. This interactive gallery will also provide a reference for galleries and museums when they are deciding whether or not to sponsor a show. Any creative professional who is interested in participating and contributing images is encouraged to visit my website, review the Call for Art section, and respond by following the guidelines.

Additional resources and references

Throughout this book, I have included many references from fields such as neuroscience, art therapy, cognitive psychology, and gerontology. If any of these references interest you, the vast majority are available online on a site called CiteULike.org (in addition to being listed at the end of this book). I've organized and sorted over 600 references by keywords/tags such as: memory, cognition, creativity, aging, culture, brain, intervention, training, and more. My references are under the following url: www.citeulike.org/user/amandaalders

Summary

There are many different ways that a creative professional can provide memory training sessions to older adults. Inviting the family into sessions and reaching out to community centers may provide opportunities for culturally sensitive services. Additionally, inter-field collaboration ensures a high quality service to older adults and consultation/referrals ensure an ethical practice. The content throughout this book has spanned many different fields and testing your knowledge before offering services to older adults is recommended.

LEARNING EVALUATION QUIZ

Name: ....   Date:...............................

Directions: The following questions are in multiple choice format. They include the words and concepts found throughout the chapter. An online version of these questions with automatic grading can be found at: www.arttherapyconsulting.com

1. A level of memory loss between normal loss with age and pathological loss from disease.
   a. Mild cognitive impairment
   b. Cognitive training
   c. Enriched environment
   d. Involuntary memories

2. A part of the brain critical for creating new memories and integrating them into a network of knowledge.
   a. Hippocampus
   b. Ageism
   c. Neurogenesis
   d. Meaning

3. A hormone produced when a person is exposed to stress.
   a. Art
   b. Ageism
   c. Cortisol
   d. Meaning

4. The creation of new neurons in the adult brain.
   a. Neuroplasticity
   b. Meaning
   c. Cortisol
   d. Neurogenesis

5. An umbrella term used for rehabilitative techniques aimed to improve cognitive functioning.
   a. Creativity
   b. Meaning
   c. Cognitive training
   d. Mild cognitive impairment

6. The aspects of the visual medium that can be manipulated and controlled to create meaning and evoke responses (e.g. line, shape, color, value, space).
   a. Serotonin
   b. Value
   c. Saturation
   d. Visual elements

7. Chemicals that transmit information from one neuron to another.
   a. Neurotransmitters
   b. Dopamine
   c. Serotonin
   d. Rorschach

8. The process of recalling and telling "stories" about people and events from the past and reporting associated thoughts and feelings.
   a. Dopamine
   b. Reminiscence
   c. Rorschach
   d. Symbiotic

9. Relative darkness or lightness of a color.
   a. Gamma
   b. Value
   c. EEG
   d. Alpha

10. The intensity of a color; how close it is to a pure hue.
    a. Stratification
    b. Serotonin
    c. Symbiotic
    d. Saturation

11. The ability to recognize, understand, and communicate the meaning of visual images.
    a. Culture
    b. Visual literacy
    c. Triadic schema
    d. Universality

12. Becoming aware of something via the senses.
    a. Connection
    b. Interpretation
    c. Perception
    d. Evaluation

13. The explanation of something which is not obvious or that does not mean the same thing to everyone.
    a. Interpretation
    b. Connection
    c. Evaluation
    d. Perception

14. The enduring behaviors, ideas, attitudes, and traditions shared by a large group of people and transmitted from one generation to the next.
    a. Connection
    b. Culture
    c. De-centering
    d. Perception

15. The meaning of a message that tells others how they should respond to the content of communication.
    a. Perception
    b. De-centering
    c. Evaluation
    d. Metamessage

16. Memory for how to do things and includes motor skills.
    a. Episodic memory
    b. Working memory
    c. Procedural memory
    d. Short-term memory

17. The neural system which includes the hippocampus and is associated with emotions and drives.
    a. Episodic memory
    b. Collages
    c. ETC
    d. Limbic system

18. Based on observed patterns; a form of thinking that involves using individual cases or particular facts to reach a general conclusion.
    a. Episodic memory
    b. Restorative strategies
    c. Amnestic MCI
    d. Inductive reasoning

19. The type of impairment which includes problems with episodic memory (verbal).
    a. Episodic memory
    b. ETC
    c. Amnestic MCI
    d. ATR-N

20. Promote recuperation; capable of returning functioning to its former state.
    a. Compensatory strategies
    b. Restorative strategies
    c. Inductive reasoning
    d. Prefrontal cortex

21. Focuses on forms and includes figure–ground differentiation.
    a. K/S or Kinesthetic/Sensory level
    b. Prefrontal cortex
    c. P/A or Perceptual/Affective level
    d. C/Sy or Cognitive/Symbolic level

22. The tendency to repeat a response inappropriately; persistent repeating of verbal or motor response, even with varied stimuli.
    a. Perseveration
    b. Referrals
    c. Neuroimaging
    d. Scope-of-practice

23. The first of a series of actions that aid in creating a sense of group identity to nourish interpersonal relationships and increase comfort. ✓
   a. Referrals
   b. Opening
   c. Neuroimaging
   d. Closing

24. Visual elements that have been associated with and correlated with specific emotional and cognitive states and traits in research.
   a. Treatment distrust
   b. Scope-of-practice
   c. Graphic indicators
   d. Adult daycares

25. Description of what a specific professional may and may not do; a set of regulations and ethical considerations.
   a. Perseveration
   b. Monochromatic
   c. Opening
   d. Scope-of-practice

26. Used to detect cognitive impairment; older adult is asked to draw a clock and set the hands at a particular time; evaluates visuospatial processing, auditory comprehension, and executive functioning.
   a. Opening
   b. Closing
   c. Adult daycares
   d. Clock Drawing Test

27. Projects that engage the entire family.
   a. Generational leveling
   b. Inter-generational projects
   c. Fine art centers
   d. Interactive/online galleries

28. A selection of images hosted online to offer dynamic opportunities for family and community members to see older adult artwork.
    a. Intergenerational projects
    b. Generational leveling
    c. Interactive/online galleries
    d. Fine art centers

29. In research, the typical duration and frequency of cognitive training.
    a. 6 weeks, 2 times a week
    b. 10 weeks, 2 times a week
    c. 6 weeks, 1 time a week
    d. 10 weeks, 1 time a week

30. Feelings based on a belief that the practices of a care provider are less than optimal due to cultural incompatibilities.
    a. Graphic indicators
    b. Referrals
    c. Treatment distrust
    d. Adult daycares

Answers:

1.a, 2.a, 3.c, 4.d, 5.c, 6.d, 7.a, 8.b, 9.b, 10.d, 11.b, 12.c, 13.a, 14.b, 15.d, 16.c, 17.d, 18.d, 19.c, 20.b, 21.c, 22.a, 23.b, 24.c, 25.d, 26.d, 27.b, 28.c, 29.d, 30.c

REFERENCES

Aanstoos, J. (2003). Visual literacy: an overview. In *32nd Applied Imagery Pattern Recognition Workshop, 2003. Proceedings*, pp.189–193. IEEE.

Abraham, R. (2004). *When words have lost their meaning: Alzheimer's patients communicate through art*. Westport, CT: Praeger.

Administration on Aging. (2011). *Minority aging*. Retrieved 10 April 2010 from www.aoa. gov/aoaroot/aging_statistics/minority_aging/Index.aspx.

Alba, R. and Islam, T. (2009). The case of the disappearing Mexican Americans: An ethnic-identity mystery. *Population Research and Policy Review, 28*(2), 109–121.

Alders, A. (2010). Moving beyond the stratification of Mexican identity through art. *Art for Life Journal, 1*(1), 49–62.

Alders, A. (2011). Perceived self-efficacy and its role in education-related cognitive performance outcomes in Latino-American elderly. *Journal of Latinos and Education, 10*(4), 299–319.

Alders, A. (2012). *The effect of art therapy on cognitive performance among ethnically diverse older adults* (unpublished dissertation). Florida State University.

Alexander, T. (1999). John Dewey and the aesthetics of human existence. In S. Rosenthal (Ed.), *Classical American pragmatism: its contemporary vitality* (pp.160–173). Urbana Champaign: University of Illinois Press.

Alzheimer's Association (2004). *Hispanics/Latinos and Alzheimer's disease*. Retrieved 1 June 2010 from www.alz.org/national/documents/report_hispanic.pdf.

Alzheimer's Association (2010a). *Alzheimer's disease facts and figures*. Retrieved 1 June 2010 from www.alz.org/documents_custom/report_alzfactsfigures2010.pdf.

Alzheimer's Association (2010b). *What is Alzheimer's?* Retrieved 3 August 2010 from www. alz.org/alzheimers_disease_what_is_alzheimers.asp.

American Psychological Association. (2010). *Guidelines for psychological practice with older adults*. Retrieved 3 August 2010 www.apa.org/practice/guidelines/older-adults.pdf.

Anderson, T. (1995). Toward a cross-cultural approach to art criticism. *Studies in Art Education, 36*(4), 198–209.

Anderson, T. and Milbrandt, M. (2005). *Art for life: Authentic instruction in art*. Burr Ridge, IL: McGraw-Hill.

Andrade, J. (2010). What does doodling do? *Applied Cognitive Psychology 24*(1), 100–106. Retrieved 12 July 2013 from http://pignottia.faculty.mjc.edu/math134/homework/doodlingCaseStudy.pdf.

Angus, J. and Reeve, P. (2006). Ageism: A threat to aging well in the 21st century. *Journal of Applied Gerontology, 25*(2), 137–152.

Aranda, M. P., Villa, V. M., Trejo, L., Ramirez, R., and Ranney, M. (2003). El Portal Latino Alzheimer's Project: Model program for Latino caregivers of Alzheimer's disease-affected people. *Social Work, 48*(2), 259–271.

Armstrong, K., Rose, A., Peters, N., Long, J., McMurphy, S., and Shea, J. (2006). Distrust of the health care system and self-reported health in the United States. *Journal of General Internal Medicine, 21*(4), 292–297.

Arnheim, R. (2004). Visual thinking. Berkeley: University of California Press.

Azeemi, S. T. and Raza, M. (2005). A critical analysis of chromotherapy and its scientific evolution. *Evidence-Based Complementary and Alternative Medicine, 2*(4), 481–488.

Ball, K., Berch, D. B., Helmers, K. F., Jobe, J. B., Leveck, M. D., Marsiske, M. for the ACTIVE Study Group. (2002). Effects of cognitive training interventions with older adults: A randomized controlled trial. *JAMA, 288*(18), 2271–2281.

Bang, M. (1991). *Picture this: Perception and composition.* Boston: Little, Brown.

Bar-On, R., Tranel, D., Denburg, N. L., and Bechara, A. (2003). Exploring the neurological substrate of emotional and social intelligence. *Brain, 126*(8), 1790–1800.

Barron, A. and Warga, M. (2007). Acquisitional pragmatics: Focus on foreign language learners. Intercultural Pragmatics, *4*(2), 113–127.

Baune, B., Suslow, T., Engelien, A., Arolt, V., and Berger, K. (2006). The association between depressive mood and cognitive performance in an elderly general population—The MEMO study. *Dementia and Geriatric Cognitive Disorders, 22,* 142–149.

Becker, D. (2000). The Mental Status Exam. *JAMA: The Journal of the American Medical Association, 283*(9), 1114.

Berk, M. and Schur, C. (2001). The effect of fear on access to care among undocumented Latino immigrants. *Journal of Immigrant Health, 3*(3), 151–156.

Berleant, A. (1964). The sensuous and the sensual in aesthetics. *Journal of Aesthetics and Art Criticism, 23*(2)185–192.

Bermudez, D. and ter Maat, M. (2006). Art therapy with Hispanic clients: Results of a survey study. *Art Therapy: Journal of the American Art Therapy Association, 24*(4), 165–171.

Berumen, L. C., Rodríguez, A., Miledi, R., and García-Alcocer, G. (2012). Serotonin receptors in hippocampus. *The Scientific World Journal,* 2012: 1–15. Rerieved 12 July 2013 from www.hindawi.com/journals/tswj/2012/823493.

Blanchard-Fields, F. (2007). Everyday problem solving and emotion. *Current Directions in Psychological Science, 16*(1), 26–31.

Boron, J. B., Turiano, N. A., Willis, S. L., and Schaie, K. W. (2007). Effects of cognitive training on change in accuracy in inductive reasoning ability. *The Journals of Gerontology Series B: Psychological Sciences and Social Sciences, 62*(3), 179–186.

Borrayo, E. A., Goldwaser, G., Vacha-Haase, T., and Hepburn, K. W. (2007). An inquiry into Latino caregivers' experience caring for older adults with Alzheimer's disease and related dementias. *Journal of Applied Gerontology, 26*(5), 486–505.

Bracey, T. and Dorn, C.M. (2001). Mind in art: Cognitive foundations in art education. *Studies in Art Education, 42*(4), 366–371.

Bransford, J. D., Brown, A. L., and Cocking, R. R. (2000). *How people learn: Brain, mind, experience, and school.* Washington, DC: National Research Council.

Braverman, E. (2005). *The edge effect: Achieve total health and longevity with the balanced brain advantage.* New York, NY: Sterling.

Brinck, I. (2007). Situated cognition, dynamic systems, and art: On artistic creativity and aesthetic experience. *Janus Head, 9*(2), 407–431.

Brinkman, D. J. (2010). Teaching creatively and teaching for creativity. *Arts Education Policy Review, 111*(2), 48–50.

Butler, R. (1980). The life review: An unrecognized bonanza. *The International Journal of Aging and Human Development, 12*(1), 35–38.

Butters, M. A., Becker, J. T., Nebes, R. D., Zmuda, M. D., Mulsant, B. H., Pollock, B. G., and Reynolds, C. F. (2000). Changes in cognitive functioning following treatment of late-life depression. *The American Journal of Psychiatry, 157*(12), 1949–1954.

Caine, G. and Caine, R. (2006). Meaningful learning and the executive functions of the brain. *New Directions for Adult and Continuing Education, 110*, 53–61.

Calisch, A. (2003). Multicultural training in art therapy: Past, present, and future. *Art Therapy: Journal of the American Art Therapy Association, 20*(1), 11–15.

Campbell, R. L. (1999). Ayn Rand and the cognitive revolution in psychology. *Journal of Ayn Rand Studies, 1*(1), 107–134. Retrieved 8 August 2010 from http://myweb.clemson.edu/~campber/randcogrev.html.

Cann, A., Calhoun, L. G., Tedeschi, R. G., Kilmer, R. P., Gil-Rivas, V., Vishnevsky, T., and Danhauer, S. C. (2009). The core beliefs inventory: a brief measure of disruption in the assumptive world. *Anxiety, Stress and Coping, 23*(1), 19–34.

Carruthers, D. (2007). The politics and ecology of indigenous folk art in Mexico. *Journal of the Society for Applied Anthropology, 60*(4), 356–366.

Carruthers, P. (2007). *The Creative-Action Theory of Creativity.* Retrieved 11 August 2013 from www.philosophy.dept.shef.ac.uk/AHRB/Project/Papers/CarruthersV3ppr.pdf.

Chamberlain, A. (2007). *How does art, analogy, and mental imagery aid in cognitive development?* Retrieved 12 February 2010 from http://archives.evergreen.edu/masterstheses/Accession89-10MIT/Chamberlain_A%20MITthesis%202007.pdf.

Chamorro-Premuzic, T. and Furnham, A. (2005). Art judgment: A measure related to both personality and intelligence? *Imagination, Cognition and Personality, 24*(1), 3–24.

Charles, S. T., Mather, M., and Carstensen, L. L. (2003). Aging and emotional memory: The forgettable nature of negative images for older adults. *Journal of Experimental Psychology: General, 132*(2), 310–324.

Chauvin, B. (2003). Visual or media literacy? *Journal of Visual Literacy, 23*(2), (Autumn), 119–129.

Chertkow, H., Verret, L., and Bergmen, H. (2001). *Predicting progression to dementia in elderly subjects with Mild Cognitive Impairment: A multidisciplinary approach.* Plenary Session, 53rd Annual Meeting of the American Academy of Neurology, Philadelphia, PA.

Chow, J. C., Auh, E. Y., Scharlach, A. E., Lehning, A. J., and Goldstein, C. (2010). Types and sources of support received by family caregivers of older adults from diverse racial and ethnic groups. *Journal of Ethnic and Cultural Diversity in Social Work, 19*(3), 175–194.

Chudler, E. (2013). *Neurotransmitters and neuroactive peptides.* Retrieved 12 July 2013 from http://faculty.washington.edu/chudler/chnt1.html.

Cohen, G. (2006). Research on creativity and aging: The positive impact of the arts on health and illness. *Generations, 30*(1), 7–15.

Cole, M. G. and Dendukuri, N. (2003). Risk factors for depression among elderly community subjects: A systematic review and meta-analysis. *American Journal of Psychiatry, 160*(6), 1147–1156.

Comas-Dias, L. (2006). Latino healing: The integration of ethnic psychology into psychotherapy. *Psychotherapy: Theory, Research, Practice, Training, 43*(4), 436–453.

Connell, C. M., Scott Roberts, J., and McLaughlin, S. J. (2007). Public opinion about Alzheimer's disease among Blacks, Hispanics, and Whites: Results from a national survey. *Alzheimer Disease and Associated Disorders, 21*(3), 232–240.

Corbie-Smith, G., Thomas, S. B., and St. George, D. M. (2002). Distrust, race, and research. *Arch Intern Med, 162*(21), 2458–2463.

Cornwell, B., Laumann, E. O., and Schumm, L. P. (2008). The social connectedness of older adults: A national profile. *American Sociological Review, 73*(2), 185–203.

Couch, J. B. (1997). Behind the veil: Mandala drawings by dementia patients. *Art Therapy: Journal of the American Art Therapy Association, 14*(3), 187–193.

Cowan, P. (1999). Drawn into the community: Re-considering the artwork of Latino adolescents. *Visual Sociology, 14*(1), 91–101.

Craig, D. and Paraiso, J. (2009). Dual diaspora and barrio art: Art as an avenue for learning English. *Journal for Learning through the Arts, 4*(1). Retrieved 1 June 2006 from http://escholarship.org/uc/item/7r0983p5.

Cummings, J. L., Miller, B. L., Christensen, D. D., and Cherry, D. (2008). Creativity and dementia: Emerging diagnostic and treatment methods for Alzheimer's disease. *CNS Spectrums, 13*(2 Suppl 2), 1–20.

Cummings, S. (2003). The efficacy of an integrated group treatment program for depressed assisted living residents. *Research on Social Work Practice, 13*(5), 608–621.

Cunia, E. (2005). Behavioral learning theory. *Principles of Instruction and Learning: A Web Quest.* Retrieved 17 August 2010 from http://erincunia.com/portfolio/MSportfolio/ide621/ide621f03production/learningtheory.htm.

Czeh, B., and Lucassen, P. (2007). What causes the hippocampal volume decrease in depression? *European Archives of Psychiatry and Clinical Neuroscience, 257*(5), 250–260.

Dalebroux, A., Goldstein, T., and Winner, E. (2008). Short-term mood repair through art-making: Positive emotion is more effective than venting. *Motivation and Emotion, 32*(4):288–295. Retrieved 25 November 2009 from https://bing.bc.edu/ellen-winner/pdf/shorttermmoodrepair.pdf.

Davidson, R. J. (2003). Affective neuroscience and psychophysiology: Toward a synthesis. *Psychophysiology, 40*(5), 655–665.

Delahaye, B. L. and Ehrich, L. C. (2008). Complex learning preferences and strategies of older adults. *Educational Gerontology, 34*(8), 649–662.

De Petrillo, L. and Winner, E. (2005). Does art improve mood? A test of a key assumption underlying art therapy. *American Journal of Art Therapy, 22*(4), 28–56.

Depp, C. A. and Jeste, D. V. (2009). Definitions and predictors of successful aging: A comprehensive review of larger quantitative studies. *Focus, 7*(1), 137–150.

Dewey, J. (1957). *Art as experience.* London: Penguin.

Diamond, K. (2000). *Older brains and new connections.* San Luis Obispo, CA: Davidson Publications.

Diamond, M. (2001). *Response of the brain to enrichment.* Retrieved 12 July 2013 from http://education.jhu.edu/newhorizons/Neurosciences/articles/Response%20of%20the%20Brain%20to%20Enrichment/index.html.

Dimond, M. (1981). Bereavement and the elderly: a critical review with implications for nursing practice and research. *Journal of Advanced Nursing, 6*(6), 461–470.

Dingfelder, S. (2005). Closing the gap for Latino patients: Research offers insights on ways psychologists can better serve one of America's fastest-growing minority populations. *Monitor on Psychology, 36*(1), 56–60.

Eisenberger, N. and Lieberman, M. (2004). Why rejection hurts: a common neural alarm system for physical and social pain. *Trends in Cognitive Sciences, 8*(7), 294–300.

Eisenberger, R. and Shanock, L. (2003). Rewards, intrinsic motivation, and creativity: A case study of conceptual and methodological isolation. *Creativity Research Journal, 15*(2), 121–130.

Eknoyan, D. (2012). The clock drawing task: Common errors and functional neuroanatomy. *Journal of Neuropsychiatry, 24*(3), 260+.

Elias, J. W. and Wagster, M. V. (2007). Developing context and background underlying cognitive intervention/training studies in older populations. *The Journals of Gerontology Series B: Psychological Sciences and Social Sciences, 62*(Special Issue 1), 5–10.

Epstein, R. (1991). Skinner, creativity, and the problem of spontaneous behavior. *Psychological Science, 2*(6), 362–370.

Epstein, R. (2002). *Consciousness, art and the brain: Lessons from Marcel Proust Consciousness and Cognition.* Retrieved 12 February 2010 from http://citeseerx.ist.psu.edu/viewdoc/download?doi=10.1.1.104.2759&rep=rep1&type=pdf.

Ertmer, P. A. and Newby, T. J. (1993). Behaviorism, cognitivism, constructivism: Comparing critical features from an instructional design perspective. *Performance Improvement Quarterly, 6*(4), 50–70.

Fann, J., Uotomoto, J., and Katon, W. (2001). Cognitive improvement with treatment of depression following mild traumatic brain injury. *The Journal of Psychosomatic Medicine, 42*, 48–52.

Felten, P. (2008). *Visual literacy.* Retrieved 25 November 2009 from http://facstaff.unca.edu/nruppert/2009/Visual%20Literacy/DigitalLiteracy/VL.pdf.

Fisher, B. (1999). Successful aging and creativity in later life. *Journal of Aging Studies, 13*(4), 457–472.

Franquiz, M. E. and Brochin-Ceballos, C. (2006). Cultural citizenship and visual literacy: US-Mexican children constructing cultural identities along the US-Mexico border. *Multicultural Perspectives, 8*(1), 5–12.

Freedberg, D. and Gallese, V. (2007). Motion, emotion and empathy in esthetic experience. *Trends in Cognitive Sciences, 11*(5), 197–203.

Furnham, A. and Chamorropremuzic, T. (2004). Personality, intelligence, and art. *Personality and Individual Differences, 36*(3), 705–715.

Fuster, J. M. (2003). *Cortex and mind: Unifying cognition.* New York: Oxford University Press.

Gallagher-Thompson, D., Solano, N., Coon, D., and Arean, P. (2003). Recruitment and retention of Latino dementia family caregivers in intervention research: Issues to face, lessons to learn. *The Gerontologist, 43*(1), 45–51.

Gallos, J. (2008). *Artful teaching: Using the visual, creative and performing arts in contemporary management education.* Retrieved 3 August 2013 from www.joangallos.com/wp-content/uploads/2008/03/artful-teaching.doc.

Gauthier, S., Reisberg, B., Zaudig, M., Petersen, R. C., Ritchie, K., Broich, K., […] International Psychogeriatric Association Expert Conference on Mild Cognitive Impairment. (2006). Mild cognitive impairment. *Lancet, 367*(9518), 1262–1270.

Geary, J. (2011). *I is an other: The secret life of metaphor and how it shapes the way we see the world.* New York: Harper Publications.

Gilley, W., Wilson, L., Bienias, L., Bennett, A., and Evans, A. (2004). Predictors of depression symptoms in persons with Alzheimer's disease. *Journal of Gerontology: Psychological Sciences, 59*(2), 75–83.

Glei, D. A., Landau, D. A., Goldman, N., Chuang, Y.-L., Rodriguez, G., and Weinstein, M. (2005). Participating in social activities helps preserve cognitive function: An analysis of a longitudinal, population-based study of the elderly. *International Journal of Epidemiology, 34*(4), 864–871.

Goldschmidt, G. (2003). The backtalk of self-generated sketches. *Design Changes, 19*, 72–73, 80.

Grady, C. L. (2008). Cognitive neuroscience of aging. *Annals of the New York Academy of Sciences, 1124*(1), 127–144.

Graham, R. E., Ahn, A. C., Davis, R. B., O'Connor, B. B., Eisenberg, D. M., and Phillips, R. S. (2005). Use of complementary and alternative medical therapies among racial and ethnic minority adults: Results from the 2002 National Health Interview Survey. *Journal of the National Medical Association, 97*(4), 535–545.

Gray, J., Braver, T., and Raichle, M. (2002). Integration of emotion and cognition in the lateral prefrontal cortex. *Proceedings of the National Academy of Science, 99*(6), 4115–4120.

Greaves, C. J. and Farbus, L. (2006). Effects of creative and social activity on the health and well-being of socially isolated older people: Outcomes from a multi-method observational study. *The Journal of the Royal Society for the Promotion of Health, 126*(3), 134–142.

Grey, A. (2013). *How art evolves consciousness.* Blog post. Retrieved 12 July 2013 from http://alexgrey.com/art-evolves-consciousness.

Gutierrez, K. D. and Rogoff, B. (2003). Cultural ways of learning: Individual traits or repertoires of practice. *Educational Researcher, 32*(5), 19–25.

Hannemann, B. T. (2006). Creativity with dementia patients. Can creativity and art stimulate dementia patients positively? *Gerontology, 52*(1), 59–65.

Harlan, J. (1993). The therapeutic value of art for persons with Alzheimer's disease and related disorders. *Loss, Grief and Care, A Journal of Professional Practice, 6*(4), 99–106.

Harris, M. (2008). *Culture in the classroom: Developing cross-cultural awareness in the secondary school foreign language classroom.* Retrieved 4 August 2013 from www.pearsonlongman.com/professionaldevelopment/downloads/articles/adults-young-learners/Culture-in-the-classroom.pdf.

Hass-Cohen, N. (2003). Art therapy mind body approaches. *Progress: Family Systems Research and Therapy, 12*, 24–38.

Hass-Cohen, N. and Carr, R. (Eds.). (2008). *Art therapy and clinical neuroscience.* London, England: Jessica Kingsley Publishers.

Helen, C. and Padilla, R. (2011). *Working with elders who have dementia and Alzheimer's disease.* Retrieved 16 August 2010 from http://ot.creighton.edu/community/OT_FOR_ELDERS/3rd_Edition_Chapters/Proofs/Padilla_Chapter_20_main.pdf.

Hendrie, H. C., Albert, M. S., Butters, M. A., Gao, S., Knopman, D. S., Launer, L. J., [...] Wagster, M. V. (2006). The NIH Cognitive and Emotional Health Project. Report of the Critical Evaluation Study Committee. *Alzheimer's and Dementia: The Journal of the Alzheimer's Association, 2*(1), 12–32.

Henley, D. (2000). Blessings in disguise: Idiomatic expression as a stimulus in group art therapy with children. *Art Therapy: Journal of the American Art Therapy Association, 17*(4), 270–275.

Hevner, K. (1935). Experimental studies of the affective value of colors and lines. *Journal of Applied Psychology, 19*(4), 385–398.

Hinz, L. (2009). *Expressive therapies continuum: A framework for using art therapy.* New York: Routledge.

Hodges, H. F., Keeley, A. C., and Grier, E. C. (2001). Masterworks of art and chronic illness experiences in the elderly. *Journal of Advanced Nursing, 36*(3), 389–398.

Horlings, R. (2008). *Emotion recognition using brain activity.* Retrieved 6 November 2012 from http://www.kbs.twi.tudelft.nl/docs/MSc/2008/Horlings/thesis.pdf.

Huitt, W. (1994). Principles for using behavior modification. *Educational Psychology Interactive.* Valdosta, GA: Valdosta State University. Retrieved 28 September 2010 from www.edpsycinteractive.org/topics/behavior/behmod.html.

Huitt, W. (2003). *The information processing approach to cognition.* Retrieved 28 September 2010 from www.edpsycinteractive.org/topics/cognition/infoproc.html.

Jameson, K. (2006). Culture and cognition: What is universal about the representation of color experience? *International Journal of Clinical Monitoring and Computing, 5*(3), 293–347.

Jobe, J. B., Smith, D. M., Ball, K., Tennstedt, S. L., Marsiske, M., Willis, S. L., [...] Kleinman, K. (2001). ACTIVE: a cognitive intervention trial to promote independence in older adults. *Controlled Clinical Trials, 22*(4), 453–479.

Jolley, R. P. and Thomas, G. V. (1995). Children's sensitivity to metaphorical expression of mood in line drawings. *British Journal of Developmental Psychology, 13*(4), 335–346. Retrieved 26 February 2011 from http://onlinelibrary.wiley.com/doi/10.1111/j.2044-835X.1995.tb00684.x/abstract.

Jones, R., Chow, T., and Gatz, M. (2006). Asian Americans and Alzheimer's disease: Assimilation, culture, and beliefs. *Journal of Aging Studies, 20*(1), 11–25.

Jung, R. E., Segall, J. M., Jeremy Bockholt, H., Flores, R. A., Smith, S. M., Chavez, R. S., and Haier, R. J. (2010). Neuroanatomy of creativity. *Human Brain Mapping, 31*(3), 398–409.

Kagin, S. L. and Lusebrink, V. B. (1978). The expressive therapies continuum. *Art Psychotherapy, 5*(4), 171–180.

Kaplan, F. (2000). *Art, science and art therapy.* Philadelphia, PA: Jessica Kingsley Publishers.

Kasper, G. and Dahl, M. (1991). Research methods in interlanguage pragmatics. *Studies in Second Language Acquisition, 13*(2), 215–247.

Kempermann, G., Gast, D., and Gage, F. H. (2002). Neuroplasticity in old age: Sustained fivefold induction of hippocampal neurogenesis by long-term environmental enrichment. *Annals of Neurology, 52*(2), 135–143.

Kim, S.-H., Kim, M.-Y., Lee, J.-H., and Chun, S.-I. (2008). Art therapy outcomes in the rehabilitation treatment of a stroke patient: A case report. *Art Therapy: Journal of the American Art Therapy Association, 25*(3), 129–133.

Kimura, S., Musha, T., Kaneko, K., Nishida, K., Sekine, K., and Oh, M. (2003). *Sensitive estimation of the effectiveness of creative art therapy on demented patients by means of DIMENSION.* Retrieved 13 April 2011 from http://sciencelinks.jp/j-east/article/200422/0000200 42204A0736172.php.

Kinney, J. M. and Rentz, C. A. (2005). Observed well-being among individuals with dementia: Memories in the Making©, an art program, versus other structured activity. *American Journal of Alzheimer's Disease and Other Dementias, 20*(4), 220–227.

Kleiner-Fisman, G., Black, S. E., and Lang, A. E. (2003). Neurodegenerative disease and the evolution of art: The effects of presumed corticobasal degeneration in a professional artist. *Movement Disorders: Official Journal of the Movement Disorder Society, 18*(3), 294–302.

Kumaran, D. and Duzel, E. (2008). The hippocampus and dopaminergic midbrain: Old couple, new insights. *Neuron, 60*(2), 197–200. Retrieved 12 July 2013 from www.stanford.edu/group/memorylab/Publications/papers/SHO_NEU08_comment.pdf.

Labrecque, L. and Milne, G. (2012). Exciting red and competent blue: The importance of color in marketing. *Journal of the Academy of Marketing Science, 40*(5), 711–727.

Larrieu, S., Letenneur, L., Orgogozo, J. M., Fabrigoule, C., Amieva, H., Le Carret, N., […] Dartigues, J. F. (2002). Incidence and outcome of mild cognitive impairment in a population-based prospective cohort. *Neurology, 59*(10), 1594–1599.

Leung, A., Maddux, W., Galinsky, A., and Chiu, C. (2008). Multicultural experience enhances creativity: The when and how. *American Psychologist, 63*(3), 169–181.

Lichtenfeld, S., Elliot, A. J., Maier, M. A., and Pekrun, R. (2012). Fertile green. *Personality and Social Psychology Bulletin, 38*(6), 784–797.

Liebmann, M. (1986) *Art therapy for groups: A handbook of themes, games, and exercises.* London: Routledge.

Link, M. W., Mokdad, A. H., Stackhouse, H. F., and Flowers, N. T. (2006). Race, ethnicity, and linguistic isolation as determinants of participation in public health surveillance surveys. *Preventing Chronic Disease, 3*(1), A09.

Logsdon, R. G., McCurry, S. M., and Teri, L. (2007). Evidence-based interventions to improve quality of life for individuals with dementia. *Alzheimer's Care Today, 8*(4), 309–318.

Lopez, S. and Weisman, A. (2004). Integrating a cultural perspective in psychological test development. In R. Velasquez, L. Arellano, and B. McNeill (Eds.), *Handbook of Chicana/o psychology and mental health* (pp.129–151). Mahwah, NJ: Erlbaum.

Lu, L. (1999). Personal or environmental causes of happiness: a longitudinal analysis. *The Journal of Social Psychology, 139*(1), 79–90.

Lusebrink, V. B. (1991). A systems oriented approach to the expressive therapies—The Expressive Therapies Continuum. *The Arts in Psychotherapy, 18*(5), 395–403.

Lusebrink, V. B. (2004). Art therapy and the brain: An attempt to understand the underlying processes of art expression in therapy. *Art Therapy: Journal of the American Art Therapy Association, 21*(3), 125–135.

Lusebrink, V. B. (2010). Assessment and therapeutic application of the Expressive Therapies Continuum: Implications for brain structures and functions. *Art Therapy: Journal of the American Art Therapy Association, 27*(4), 168–177.

Lusebrink, V. B. and McGuigan, F. J. (1989). Psychophysiological components of imagery. *The Pavlovian Journal of Biological Science, 24,* 58–62.

Mahoney, D. F., Cloutterbuck, J., Neary, S., and Zhan, L. (2005). African American, Chinese, and Latino family caregivers' impressions of the onset and diagnosis of dementia: Cross-cultural similarities and differences. *The Gerontologist, 45*(6), 783–792.

Malchiodi, C. (2006). *The art therapy sourcebook.* Lincolnwood, IL: Lowell House.

Manly, J. J., Tang, M. X., Schupf, N., Stern, Y., Vonsattel, J. P., and Mayeux, R. (2008). Frequency and course of mild cognitive impairment in a multiethnic community. *Annals of Neurology, 63*(4), 494–506.

Marder-Kamhi, M. and Torres, L. (2000). Critical neglect of Ayn Rand's theory of art. *The Journal of Ayn Rand Studies, 2*(1), 1–46.

Martinez, D., Orlowska, D., Narendran, R., Slifstein, M., Liu, F., Kumar, D., Broft, A., Van Heertum, R., and Kleber, H. D. (2010). Dopamine type 2/3 receptor availability in the striatum and social status in human volunteers. *Biological Psychiatry, 67*(3), 275–278. Retrieved 12 July 2013 from http://europepmc.org/articles/PMC2812584.

Mateer, C. A., Sira, C. S., and O'Connell, M. E. (2005). Putting Humpty Dumpty together again: The importance of integrating cognitive and emotional interventions. *The Journal of Head Trauma Rehabilitation, 20*(1), 62–75.

Maurer, K., and Prvulovic, D. (2004). Paintings of an artist with Alzheimer's disease: Visuoconstructural deficits during dementia. *Journal of Neural Transmission, 111*(3), 235–245.

McNiff, S. (1992). *Art as medicine.* Boston, MA: Shambala.

Mehta, R. and Zhu, R. J. (2009). Blue or red? exploring the effect of color on cognitive task performances. *Science, 323*(5918), 1226–1229.

Mell, J. C., Howard, S. M., and Miller, B. L. (2003). Art and the brain. *Neurology, 60*(10), 1707–1710.

Mendez, M. F. (2004). Dementia as a window to the neurology of art. *Medical Hypotheses, 63*(1), 1–7.

Merriam, S. B. and Mohamad, M. (2000). How cultural values shape learning in older adulthood: The case of Malaysia. *Adult Education Quarterly, 51*(1), 45–63.

Messaris, P. (1993). Visual "literacy": A theoretical synthesis. *Communication Theory, 3*(4), 277–294.

Metcafi, E. (2010). *Black art, folk art and social control.* Retrieved 13 April 2011 from http://negroartist.com/writings/Black%20Art,%20Folk%20Art,%20and%20Social%20Control.pdf.

MetLife Foundation. (2012). *What America thinks: The MetLife Foundation Alzheimer's Survey.* Retrieved 2 May 2013 from www.metlife.com/assets/cao/contributions/foundation/2011-ml-alzheimer-awards-pr.pdf.

Miller, B. L. and Hou, C. E. (2004). Portraits of artists: Emergence of visual creativity in dementia. *Archives of Neurology, 61*(6), 842–844.

Miller, B. L., Yener, G., and Akdal, G. (2005). Artistic patterns in dementia. *Journal of Neurological Sciences (Turkish), 22*(3), 245–249.

Miller, D. B. and O'Callaghan, J. (2005). Aging, stress and the hippocampus. *Aging Research Reviews, 4*(2), 123–140.

Minckler, D. (2008). *US minority population continues to grow.* Retrieved 20 February 2011 from www.america.gov/st/peopleplace-english/2008/May/20080513175840zjsred na0.1815607.html.

Morano, C. L. and Bravo, M. (2002). A psychoeducational model for Hispanic Alzheimer's disease caregivers. *Gerontologist, 42*(1), 122–126.

Morrell, M. (2011). Signs and symbols: Art and language in art therapy. *Journal of Clinical Art Therapy, 1*(1), 25–32.

Morris, C. B. and Stuhr, P. L. (2001). Multicultural art and visual cultural education in a changing world. *Art Education, 54*(4).

Mungas, D., Reed, B. R., Farias, S. T. T., and Decarli, C. (2009). Age and education effects on relationships of cognitive test scores with brain structure in demographically diverse older persons. *Psychology and Aging, 24*(1), 116–128.

Musha, T., Kimura, S., Kaneko, K., Nishida, K., and Sekine, K. (2000). Emotion Spectrum Analysis Method (ESAM) for monitoring the effects of art therapy applied on demented patients. *CyberPsychology and Behavior, 1*(3), 441–446.

Naiman, L. (2011, 19 November). *Creativity at work.* Retrieved 30 December 2012 from www.creativityatwork.com/what-is-creativity/#.UcXzQvnVBXf.

Neville, S. (2008). Older people with delirium: worthless and childlike. *International Journal of Nursing Practice, 14*(6), 463–469.

Nevin, J. A. and Grace, R. C. (2000). Behavioral momentum and the law of effect. *Behavioral and Brain Sciences, 23*(1), 73–90.

Ormrod, J.E. (1999). *Human learning* (3rd ed.). Upper Saddle River, NJ: Prentice-Hall.

Ostbye, T., Krause, K., Norton, M., Tschanz, J., and Sanders, L. (2006). Ten dimensions of health and their relationships with overall self-reported health and survival in a predominately religiously active elderly population: The Cache County Memory Study. *Journal of the American Geriatric Society, 54*, 199–209.

Østergaard, S. (2008). Art and cognition. *Cognitive Semiotics, 2008*(3), 114–133.

Pannells, T.C. and Claxton, A. F (2008). Happiness, creative ideation, and locus of control. *Creativity Research Journal, 20*(1), 67–71.

Park, D. C., Gutchess, A. H., Meade, M. L., and Stine-Morrow, E. A. L. (2007). Improving cognitive function in older adults: Nontraditional approaches. *The Journals of Gerontology Series B: Psychological Sciences and Social Sciences, 62*(Special Issue 1), 45–52.

Pauwels, L. (2008). Visual literacy and visual culture: Reflections on developing more varied and explicit visual competencies. *The Open Communication Journal, 2*(1), 79–85.

Perneczky, R., Wagenpfeil, S., Lunetta, K. L., Cupples, L. A., Green, R. C., Decarli, C., [...] Kurz, A. (2009). Education attenuates the effect of medial temporal lobe atrophy on cognitive function in Alzheimer's disease: The MIRAGE study. *Journal of Alzheimer's Disease: JAD, 17*(4), 855–862.

Perry, B. (2008, November). *The healing arts: The neuro-develop-mental impact of art therapies.* Paper presented at the 39th Annual Conference of the American Art Therapy Association, Cleveland, OH.

Petersen, R. C. (2011). Mild cognitive impairment. *New England Journal Medicine, 364*(23), 2227–2234.

Petersen, R. C. and Negash, S. (2008). Mild cognitive impairment: An overview. *CNS Spectrums, 13*, 45–53.

Pittiglio, L. (2000). Use of reminiscence therapy in patients with Alzheimer's disease. *Lippincott's Case Management, 5*(6), 216–220.

Pizarro, J. (2004). The efficacy of art and writing therapy: Increasing positive mental health outcomes and participant retention after exposure to traumatic experience. *Journal of the American Art Therapy Association, 21*(1), 5–12.

Potter, L. M., Grealy, M. A., and O'Connor, R. C. (2009). Healthy ageing, perceived motor-efficacy, and performance on cognitively demanding action tasks. *British Journal of Psychology, 100*(1), 49–70.

Press, D., Mosha, N., Iguchi, L., Cohen, D., and Robertson, E. (2009). Procedural skill learning in Alzheimer's disease: Goal vs. action. *Alzheimer's and Dementia, 5*(4), 453.

Pruessner, J. C., Lord, C., Meaney, M., and Lupien, S. (2004). Effects of self-esteem on age-related changes in cognition and the regulation of the hypothalamic-pituitary-adrenal axis. *Annuals of the NY Academy of Science, 1032*, 186–190.

Radford, G. P. and Radford, M. L. (2005). Structuralism, post-structuralism, and the library: De Saussure and Foucault. *Journal of Documentation, 61*(1), 60–78.

Rand, A. (1969). *Romantic manifesto*. New York, NY: Signet.

Rand, A. (1971). Brief summary. *The Objectivist, 10*(9), 1–4.

Rentz, C. A. (2002). Memories in the making: Outcome-based evaluation of an art program for individuals with dementing illnesses. *American Journal of Alzheimer's Disease and Other Dementias, 17*(3), 175–181.

Reynolds, F. and Prior, S. (2006). The role of art-making in identity maintenance: case studies of people living with cancer. *European Journal of Cancer Care, 15*(4), 333–341.

Rhyne, J. (1979). Drawings as personal constructs: A study in visual dynamics. *Dissertation Abstracts International, 40*(5), 2411B. (University Microfilm International No. Tx375–487.)

Richards, M. (2004). The cognitive consequences of concealing feelings. *Current Directions in Psychological Science, 13*(4), 131–134.

Rodgers, W., Ofstedal, M., and Herzog, R. (2003). Trends in scores on tests of cognitive ability in the elderly US population, 1993–2000. *Journal of Gerontology, 58*(6), 338–346.

Rothman, S. M. and Mattson, M. P. (2010). Adverse stress, hippocampal networks, and Alzheimer's disease. *NeuroMolecular Medicine, 12*(1), 56–70.

Rubin, J. (2001). *Approaches to art therapy: Theory and technique*. New York: University Press.

Rush, J. (1987). Interlocking images: The conceptual core of a discipline-based art lesson. *Studies in Art Education, 28*(4) (Summer, 1987), 206–220. Retrieved 1 June 2010 from www.depts.ttu.edu/museumttu/CFASWebsite/5333/Supplemental%20Readings%202011/Rush_Interlocking%20Images.pdf.

Rusted, J., Sheppard, L., and Waller, D. (2006). A multi-centre randomized control group trial on the use of art therapy for older people with dementia. *Group Analysis, 39*(4), 517–536.

Samton, J., Ferrando, S., Sanelli, P., Karimi, S., Raiteri, V., and Barnhill, J. (2005). The Clock Drawing Test: Diagnostic, functional, and neuroimaging correlates in older medically ill adults. *The Journal of Neuropsychiatry and Clinical Neurosciences, 17*(4), 533–540.

Sapolsky, R. (2010). November 14. This is your brain on metaphors. *New York Times*. Retrieved 2 May 2013 from www.nytimes.com.

Sartwell, C. (2003). Aesthetics of the everyday. In J. Levinson (Ed.), *The Oxford Handbook of Aesthetics* (pp.761–770). Oxford: Oxford University Press.

Schapiro, M. (1937). *Nature of abstract art.* Retrieved 1 June 2010 from http://timothyquigley. net/vcs/schapiro-naa.pdf.

Scheibe, S. and Blanchard-Fields, F. (2009). Effects of regulating emotions on cognitive performance: What is costly for young adults is not so costly for older adults. *Psychology and Aging, 24*(1), 217–223.

Schunk, D. H. (2007). *Learning theories: An educational perspective* (5th ed.). Upper Saddle River, NJ: Pearson.

Schweitzer, L. and Stephenson, M. (2008). Charting the challenges and paradoxes of constructivism: A view from professional education. *Teaching in Higher Education, 13*(5), 583–593.

Seligman, M.E.P. (2002). *Authentic happiness: Using the new positive psychology to realize your potential for lasting fulfillment.* New York: Free Press/Simon and Schuster.

Seligman, M. E. P., Parks, A., and Steen, T. (2004). A balanced psychology and a full life. *The Royal Society, Philosophical Transactions: Biological Sciences, 359,* 1379–1381. Retrieved 1 June 2010 from www.ppc.sas.upenn.edu/balancedpsychologyarticle.pdf.

Seeman, T. E., Rodin, J., and Albert, M. (1993). Self-efficacy and cognitive performance in high-functioning older individuals: MacArthur studies of successful aging. *Journal of Aging and Health, 5*(4), 455–474.

Serrano, C., Allegri, R. F., Martelli, M., Taragano, F., and Rinalli, P. (2005). Visual art, creativity and dementia. *Vertex (Buenos Aires, Argentina), 16*(64), 418–429.

Serrano, J. P., Latorre, J. M. M., Gatz, M., and Montanes, J. (2004). Life review therapy using autobiographical retrieval practice for older adults with depressive symptomatology. *Psychology and Aging, 19*(2), 270–277.

Silver, R. (1999). Differences among aging and young adults in attitudes and cognition. *Art Therapy: Journal of the American Art Therapy Association, 16*(3), 133–139.

Silvia, P. (2005). Emotional responses to art: From collation and arousal to cognition and emotion. *Review of General Psychology, 1*(4), 342–357.

Singer, T., Verhaeghen, P., Ghisletta, P., Lindenberger, U., and Baltes, P. B. (2003). The fate of cognition in very old age: Six-year longitudinal findings in the Berlin Aging Study (BASE). *Psychology and Aging, 18*(2), 318–331.

Sitzer, D. I., Twamley, E. W., and Jeste, D. V. (2006). Cognitive training in Alzheimer's disease: A meta-analysis of the literature. *Acta Psychiatrica Scandinavica, 114*(2), 75–90.

Smallwood, J., McSpadden, M., and Schooler, J. W. (2007) The lights are on but no one's home: Meta-awareness and the decoupling of attention when the mind wanders. *Psychonomic Bulletin & Review, 14*(3), (June), 527–533.

Snowdon, D. (2001). *Aging with grace: What the Nun Study teaches us about leading longer, healthier, and more meaningful lives.* New York: Bantam Books.

Spendlove, D. (2007). A conceptualisation of emotion within art and design education: A creative, learning and product-orientated triadic schema. *International Journal of Art and Design Education, 26*(2), 155–166.

Stern, Y. (2009). Cognitive reserve. *Neuropsychologia, 47*(10), 2015–2028.

Stewart, E. G. (2004). Art therapy and neuroscience blend: Working with patients who have dementia. *Art Therapy: Journal of the American Art Therapy Association, 21*(3), 148–155.

Studenski, S., Carlson, M. C., Fillit, H., Greenough, W. T., Kramer, A., and Rebok, G. W. (2006). From bedside to bench: Does mental and physical activity promote cognitive vitality in late life? *Science of Aging Knowledge Environment, 2006*(10), 21+.

Sunderland, T., Hill, J. L., Mellow, A. M., Lawlor, B. A., Gunder-Sheimer, J., Newhouse, P. A., and Grafman, J. H. (1989). Clock drawing in Alzheimer's disease: A novel measure of dementia severity. *Journal of the American Geriatric Society, 37,* 725–729.

Sutcliffe, A., Dunbar, R., Binder, J., and Arrow, H. (2012). Relationships and the social brain: Integrating psychological and evolutionary perspectives. *British Journal of Psychology, 103*(2), 149–168. Retrieved 12 July 2013 from http://onlinelibrary.wiley.com/doi/10.1111/j.2044-8295.2011.02061.x/full.

Talamantes, M., Lindeman, R., and Mouton, C. (2010). *Ethnographic curriculum module: Health and healthcare of Hispanic/Latino American elders.* Retrieved 13 April 2011 from www.stanford.edu/group/ethnoger/hispaniclatino.html.

Thoman, D., Sansone, C., and Pasupathi, M. (2007). Talking about interests: Exploring the role of social interaction for regulating motivation and the interest experience. *Journal of Happiness Studies, 8*(3), 335–370.

Thomas, D. R. (1988). The law of effect: Contingency or contiguity. *Behavioral and Brain Sciences, 11*(3), 470–471.

Thorsen, K. (1998). The paradoxes of gerotranscendence: The theory of gerotranscendence in a cultural gerontological and post-modernist perspective. *Norwegian Journal of Epidemiology, 8*(2), 165–176. Retrieved 8 August 2013 from www.ntnu.no/ojs/index.php/norepid/article/view/464/434.

Torrance, E. P. (1965). Rewarding creative behavior; experiments in classroom creativity.

Torres, L., and Marder-Kamhi, M. (2000). *What art is: The esthetic theory of Ayn Rand.* Chicago, IL: Open Court Publishing.

Triandis, H. C. (2001). Individualism-collectivism and personality. *Journal of Personality, 69*(6), 907–924.

Tsai, A. Y., Yang, M. J., Lan, C. F., and Chen, C. S. (2008). Evaluation of the effect of cognitive intervention programs for the community-dwelling elderly with subjective memory complaints. *International Journal of Geriatric Psychiatry, 23*(11), 1172–1174.

Tulving, E. (2002). Episodic memory: From mind to brain. *Annual Review of Psychology, 53,* 1–25.

Turner, R. J. and Avison, W. R. (2003). Status variations in stress exposure: Implications for the interpretation of research on race, socioeconomic status, and gender. *Journal of Health and Social Behavior, 44*(4), 488–505.

Ueda, Y., Hayashi, K., Kuroiwa, K., Miyoshi, N., Kashiba, H., and Takeda, D. (2004). Consciousness and recognition of five colors—using functional-MRI and brain wave measurements. *Journal of International Society of Life Information Science, 22,* 366–371.

Ueno, A., Abe, N., Suzuki, M., Shigemune, Y., Hirayama, K., Mori, E., [...] Fujii, T. (2009). Reactivation of the medial temporal lobe and visual association areas during the retrieval of visual information: A Positron Emission Tomography study. *NeuroImage, 47,* S75.

University of California. (2007, 24 January). Learning slows physical progression of Alzheimer's disease. *ScienceDaily.* Retrieved 1 June 2010 from www.sciencedaily.com/releases/2007/01/070123182024.htm.

Valentijn, S. A. M., Hill, R. D., Van Hooren, S. A. H., Bosma, H., *et al.* (2006). Memory self-efficacy predicts memory performance: Results from a 6-year follow-up study. *Psychology and Aging, 21*(1), 165–172.

Van Gerven, P. (2002). Cognitive load theory and aging: Effects of worked examples on training efficiency. *Learning and Instruction, 12*(1), 87–105.

Vanlierde, A. and Wanet-Defalque, M.-C. (2005). The role of visual experience in mental imagery. *Journal of Visual Impairment and Blindness, 99*(3), 165–178.

Verdugo, R. (2009). Racial stratification, social consciousness, and the education of Mexican Americans in Fabens, Texas: A socio-historical case study. *Spaces for Difference: An Interdisciplinary Journal, 1*(2). Retrieved on 20 November 2010 from www.escholarship.org/uc/item/3bk1q2dq.

Vulchanova, M., Vulchanov, V., and Stankova, M. (2011) *Idiom comprehension in the first language: A developmental study.* Vigo International Journal of Applied Linguistics. Retrieved 4 May 2013 from http://webs.uvigo.es/vialjournal/pdf/Vial-2011-Article8.pdf.

Wagle, A., Berrios, G., and Ho, L. (1999). The cognitive failures questionnaire in psychiatry. *Comprehensive Psychiatry, 40*(6), 478–484.

Weisberg, R. (2010). The study of creativity: From genius to cognitive science. *International Journal of Cultural Policy, 16*(3), 235–253.

Welsch, W. (1999). *Richard Rorty: Philosophy beyond argument and truth?* Retrieved 12 August 2013 from http://sammelpunkt.philo.at:8080/193/1/Rorty.html.

Whitbourne, S. (2010). Creativity and successful brain aging: Going with the flow. *Psychology Today.* Retrieved 13 April 2011 from www.psychologytoday.com/blog/fulfillment-any-age/201003/creativity-and-successful-brain-aging-going-the-flow.

Williams, L. M., Brown, K. J., Palmer, D., Liddell, B. J., Kemp, A. H., Olivieri, G., [...] Gordon, E. (2006). The mellow years? Neural basis of improving emotional stability over age. *The Journal of Neuroscience, 26*(24), 6422–6430.

Willis, S. L., Tennstedt, S. L., Marsiske, M., Ball, K., Elias, J., Koepke, K. M., [...] Wright, E. (2006). Long-term effects of cognitive training on everyday functional outcomes in older adults. *JAMA, 296*(23), 2805–2814.

Wilson, R. S., Krueger, K. R., Arnold, S. E., Schneider, J. A., Kelly, J. F., Barnes, L. L., Tang, Y., and Bennett, D. A. (2007). Loneliness and risk of Alzheimer disease. *Archives of General Psychiatry, 64*(2), 234–240.

Wilson, A. and Ross, M. (2003). The identity function of autobiographical memory: Time is on our side. *Memory, 11*(2), 137–149.

Winner, E. (2007). Visual thinking in arts education: Homage to Rudolf Arnheim. *Psychology of Aesthetics, Creativity, and the Arts, 1*(1), 25–31.

Wood, A. H. and Alberta, A. J. (2009). A community-driven behavioral health approach for older adults: Lessons learned. *Journal of Community Psychology, 37*(5), 663–669.

Woods, D., Spector, A., Jones, C., Orrell, M., and Davies, S. (2009). Reminiscence therapy for dementia. *Cochrane Database of Systematic Reviews, 18*(2). doi: 10.1002/14651858. CD001120.pub2.

Woolhiser-Stallings, J. (2010). Collage as a therapeutic modality for reminiscence in patients with dementia. *Art Therapy: Journal of the American Art Therapy Association, 27*(3), 136–140.

Yamagami, T., Oosawa, M., Ito, S., and Yamaguchi, H. (2007). Effect of activity reminiscence therapy as brain-activating rehabilitation for elderly people with and without dementia. *Psychogeriatrics, 7*(2), 69–75.

Ybarra, O., Burnstein, E., Winkielman, P., Keller, M. C., Manis, M., Chan, E., and Rodriguez, J. (2008). Mental exercising through simple socializing: Social interaction promotes general cognitive functioning. *Personality and Social Psychology Bulletin, 34*(2), 248–259.

Yevin, I. (2006). Ambiguity in art. *Complexus, 3*(1–3), 74–82.

Yoto, A., Katsuura, T., Iwanaga, K., and Shimomura, Y. (2007). Effects of object color stimuli on human brain activities in perception and attention referred to EEG alpha band response. *Journal of Physiological Anthropology, 26*(3), 373–379. Retrieved 12 July 2013 from http://photometry.kriss.re.kr/wiki/img_auth.php/2/2b/JPSA_26_373_(2007). pdf.

Zock, M., and Rapp, R. (2010). *Cognitive aspects of the lexicon.* Retrieved 4 May 2013 http://aclweb.org/anthology//W/W12/W12-5100.pdf.

SUBJECT INDEX

Page numbers in *italics* refer to figures and tables.

AATA (American Art Therapy Association) *159*, 160
acetylcholine 47, *48*, 52–3, *53*, 55, 56, *57*, *58*, 59, 125
achievement, and creative thought *32*, 33
acupuncture 55
adaptability 27
adrenaline *51*
adult daycare 91, 142, 145–6, *146*
aesthetic experiences 27, *42*, 43, 124, 126
affection, physical 69, 71
African-American culture 28, 67, 68
ageism, overcoming 17–18, *19*
aging process 19, *20*, 114, 125–6
alpha brain waves 47, 48–50, *48*, *49*, 55, 56, 57, *57*, *58*, 59, 121, 122
Alzheimer's disease (AD) 15, 20–1, 40, 65, 100
American Art Therapy Association (AATA) *159*, 160
amnestic MCI 88
anxiety 22–3, 28, 34, 73, 116, 136, 149
art
    in communication 75–6, *76*
    definition 27
    social sharing of meaning through 78–82
        evaluation and connection 81–2
        interpretation 80
        perception 79
art classes 136–7
art-making
    in groups 59–61, *60*
    and inductive reasoning 99
    understanding cerebral activity in 104–5
    and verbal episodic memory 100
    and visual search and identification 98–9
art sessions
    additional planning for effective sessions 116–18, *118*
    content *101*
    duration 114

elements of successful sessions 114–15
        example plans *115*
        timeline *116*
    frequency 114
    rhythmic structure and versatility in directives 118–19
    ten weeks of sessions: conclusion 133–4
    ten weeks of sessions: outline 120–9
        week one and two: creative behavior during K/ S 120–2, *122*
        week three and four: creative thought during P/ A 122–4, *123*
        week five and six: creative self-expression for C/ Sy 124–6, *125*
        week seven and eight: P/ A level revisited 126–8, *127*
        week nine and ten: K/ S level revisited 128–9, *128*
    ten weeks of sessions: single directive 129–33
        C/ Sy directives 131–2
        K/ S directives 130, 133
        P/ A directives 131, 132–3
art shows 133–4
art supplies list 160
art therapy 11–12, 43, 44, 45, 86, 87, 92, 104–5, 136–7, 152
Art Therapy Relational Neuroscience Principles *see* ATR-N
art viewing 99, *99*–100, *100*–1
artistic creativity 14, 16, *16*, 24
arts for health 86, 136
artwork
    examples and corresponding ETC 105–8, *106*, *107*, *108*
    steps to producing 32–3
Asian culture 28, 67, 68, 138, 139
assisted living facilities 142, 145–6, *146*
assumptive worlds 66, 68, *69*, 70
ATR-N (Art Therapy Relational Neuroscience Principles) 104–5, 108, *108*, 120, 130
attention deficit 91, 97
autonomous nervous system 86, 104, 108

Beck Depression Inventory 158
bereavement 24
beta-amyloid protein 88
beta brain waves 47, *48*, 50–2, *51*, 55, 56, 57,
    57, *58*, 59, 123
black (color) 75, 133
black (culture) 62–3, 139, 154
blood flow, through the brain 20, *48*
blue 54–6, 75, 131
bodily pleasures 42–3, *42*, 48–50, *49*, 120–1
brain atrophy 153, *154*
brain cells 19, 20, 21, 26
brain, the *see* happiness, social creativity, and
    the brain; neurobiology of creativity and
    expressivity; *parts of the brain*
brain waves 46–7, *46*
    see also neurotransmitters and creativity
brainstorming 43, *51*, 55
breathing *49*, 86, 104, 105, 120, 145

C/ Sy (Cognitive/ Symbolic) level of ETC
    creative self-expression for 124–6, *125*
    directives 131–2
    example of artwork 106–7, *107*
    and learning frameworks *109*, 111, *111*,
        112
care
    cultural trends in seeking 138–9
        distrust of medical care 138–9
    self-care 24
    services/ systems across settings 142–6,
        146
        adult daycare vs. assisted living facilities
            145–6, *146*
        holistic and community centers 144–5,
            144
        museums and galleries 143
caregivers 139–40
Caucasian culture 103, 139
CFQ (Cognitive Failures Questionnaire) 158
childhood memories 99, 119, *125*, 126
Chinese culture 55, *74*
chromotherapy 55
churches, openings and closings to services
    117
CiteULike.org 161
Clock Drawing Test (CDT) 153–4, *154*,
    156–7, *157*
closings, to art sessions 116–18, *118*
cognitive abilities, addressing 83–5
"cognitive architecture" 31, 43
Cognitive Failures Questionnaire (CFQ) 158
cognitive impairment 87–92
    attention deficit 91
        graphic indicators linked to 156–7, *157*
    language disturbance 88–9

memory 92
    motor coordination 90–1
    perception 91–2
    visuospatial skills 89–90, *90*
cognitive performance, targeting through
    creativity 85–7
cognitive reserve 94
Cognitive/ Symbolic level of ETC *see* C/ Sy
cognitive training through creative self-
    expression 83–112
    addressing cognitive abilities 83–5
    cognitive training 94–7
        compensatory strategies 96–7
        restorative strategies 95–6
    educational vs. therapeutic frameworks
        108–12, *109*, *110*, *111*, *112*
    emotion-focused interventions 85–7
        targeting cognitive performance through
            creativity 85–7
    expressivity-based memory techniques
        97–102, *98*
        inductive reasoning 99–100
        verbal episodic memory 100–2, *101*
        visual search and identification 98–9
    nature of cognitive impairment 87–92
        attention deficit 91
        language disturbance 88–9
        memory 92
        motor coordination 90–1
        perception 91–2
        visuospatial skills 89–90, *90*
    neurobiology of creativity and expressivity
        102–3, *102*
    theory: going beyond "recipes" 103–8
        examples of artwork and corresponding
            ETC 105–8, *106*, *107*, *108*
        understanding cerebral activity in art-
            making 104–5
    type of memory impacted 93–4
        procedural vs. declarative 93–4
        short-term working memory vs. long-
            term memory 93
    see also memory training
collaboration 84, 136
collages 96, 98–9, *101*, *116*, 123–4, *123*
collectivist cultures 103–4, 138
color 54–6, 75, 119, 131–3
color therapy 55
communication 72–6, *74*
    art in 75–6, *76*
    interpersonal 84
    non-verbal 26, 67, 72–3
community centers 129, 138, 142, 144–5,
    146
community collaborations 135–62
    additional resources and references 161

community collaborations *cont.*
  caregivers 139–40
  cultural trends in seeking care 138–9
    distrust of medical care 138–9
  getting started 147–51
    intake forms *148*, *150–1*
    understanding the needs of the older
      adult participants 147–9
  identifying symptoms cross-culturally
    152–8
    Clock Drawing Test 153–4, *154*, 156–7,
      157
    graphic indicators linked to cognitive
      impairment 156–7, *157*
    understanding older adult self-perceived
      memory functioning 157–8
  inter-generational projects 140–1, *141*, *142*
  organizations 158–60, *159*
  scope-of-practice 136–7
  services/ systems of care across settings
    142–6
    adult daycare vs. assisted living facilities
      145–6, *146*
    holistic and community centers 144–5,
      144
    museums and galleries 143
  ways to continue learning 161
compassion 52, 81, 125, 129
compensatory strategies, in cognitive training
    96–7
confidence 32–5, *32*, 84, 108–9, 133–4
connection 81–2, *98*
constructional praxis 90
cool colors 55, 131
cortical thickness 102–3, *102*
cortisol 22, 23
counseling 86
creative behavior
  cueing *29*, 30–1
  guided steps 29–30, *29*
  during K/ S 120–2, *122*, 128–9, *128*,
    130, 133
  modeling *29*, 30
  pattern recognition *29*, 31
  reinforcement *29*, 30
creative self-expression 35–7, *36*
  for C/ Sy 124–6, *125*, 131–2
  everyday experiences 37
  meaning and symbolism 37
  negotiated perspectives 37
  personal interpretations 36
  self-reflection 36
creative thought 31–5, *32*
  achievement 33
  effort and persistence 32–3
  evaluation 34

joy 32
  observation 34
  during P/ A 122–4, *123*, 126–8, *127*, 131,
    132–3
  reaction 34–5
  standards and goals 33
creativity
  domains and *16*
  for enhanced cognitive performance 14–15
  incorporating into older adult identity
    through art-making 27–37
    creative behavior 29–31, *29*
    creative self-expression 35–7, *36*
    creative thought 31–5, *32*
  neurobiology of 102–3
cross-cultural identification of symptoms
  Clock Drawing Test 153–4, *154*, 156–7,
    157
  graphic indicators linked to cognitive
    impairment 156–7, *157*
  identifying 152–8
  understanding older adult self-perceived
    memory functioning 157–8
CT *see* cognitive training
Cuban culture 107, *107*
cueing *29*, 30–1
culture 66–72, 84, 103–4, 117
  providing cultural neutrality 68–71, *69*, *70*
  rules that may promote positive outcomes
    with older adults 71–2
  see also individual cultures

de-centering techniques 70–1, *70*
declarative memory 93–4, 121
depression
  advantages of emotion-focused techniques
    40
  indicators 25, 158
  negative impact of 16, 114
  and social isolation 23–4, 103
  use of doodling 58
Dharma Studio, Coconut Grove, FL 144–5,
    144
difficulty, linear model of 108–9, *109*
domains, and artistic creativity *16*
doodling 58–9
dopamine 47, *48*, 50–2, *51*, 55, 56, 57, *57*,
    58, 59, 60, 123
duration, of art sessions 114

e-courses 161
educational vs. therapeutic frameworks, in
    cognitive training 108–12, *109*, *110*,
    111, *112*
EEG (electroencephalography) 44–6, *45*
effort, and creative thought 32–3, *32*

Egyptian culture 55
electro-chemical processes 45–6, 55
electroencephalography (EEG) 44–6, *45*
emotion-focused interventions 40, 85–7, 127, *127*
emotional health 25
English culture *74*
English language 75, 97
enriched environments 22, 26
episodic memory 93, 94, *98*, 100–2, *101*
ETC (Expressive Therapies Continuum)
    examples of artwork 105–8, *106, 107*
    in an holistic session 145
    openings and closings to sessions 116–18, *118*
    rhythmic structure and versatility in directives 118–19
    ten weeks of sessions: conclusion 133–4
    ten weeks of sessions: outline 120–9
    ten weeks of sessions: single directive 129–33
    tenet *108*
    as a therapeutic framework 108–12, *109, 111, 112*
evaluation
    and connection 81–2
    and creative thought *32*, 34
everyday experiences *36*, 37
executive functioning *see* higher order pleasures
explanatory models 68–70, *69*
explicit memory 93–4, 121
Expressive Therapies Continuum *see* ETC
expressivity, neurobiology of *102*
expressivity-based memory techniques 97–102, *98*
    inductive reasoning 99–100
    verbal episodic memory 100–2, *101*
    visual search and identification 98–9

families, topics to engage *141, 142*
fatigue, mental 110, *111*
feedback, positive 25, 29
"fight, flight, or freeze" response 18
figurative language 72, 73–5, *74*, 124
figure–ground perception 90, *90*, 122–3
folk healing 28, 67, 138
frequency, of art sessions 114

galleries *see* museums and galleries
gamma brain waves 47, *48*, 52–3, *53*, 55, 56, *57, 58*, 59, 125
General Health Questionnaire 158
geometrical shapes 57
gero-expressivity 17
gesso 130

goals, and creative thought *32*, 33
graphic indicators, linked to cognitive impairment 152, 156–7, *157*
gratifications *42*, 44, 52
green 131
grief 24

Haitian culture 62–3
hand–eye coordination 48, *49*
happiness, social creativity, and the brain 39–63, 44–7, *45, 46*
    combining visual elements for enhanced mood 58–61
    art-making in groups 59–61, *60*
    happiness and creative self-expression 40–4
    elevating mood during creative sessions 41–4, *42*
    happiness, creativity, and the brain 44–7, *45, 46*
    making art that expresses and enhances mood 53–8
    visual elements, cognition, and mood 54–8, *57, 58*
    neurotransmitters and creativity 47–53
    acetylcholine 52–3, *53*
    dopamine 50–2, *51*
    neurotransmitters, brain waves, and memory training *48*
    serotonin 48–50, *49*
    social equality vs. stratification during creativity and happiness 61–3
healing, power of art to heal 104
healthcare, distrust of US system 138–9, 152
heart-rate 86, 104, 120
here-and-now experiences 23, 42–3, 48, 119, 120, 122
hierarchical inclusion 69–70, *69*, 71
higher order pleasures *42*, 43, 50, 99, 123
hippocampus 19, 20, *20*, 21, 22, 40, 50, 51, 88, 100, 103
Hispanic culture 62–3, 67–8, *74*, 103, 138, 139
holistic centers 129, 144–5, *144, 146*
homogenous groups 62, 68
hue (color) 56

idioms 73–4, *74*
IEATA (International Expressive Arts Therapy Association) *159*
imagery 73, 76
implicit memory 93, 94, 99, 120
independent living 96, 97
individualistic cultures 103, 104
inductive reasoning 96, 97, *98*, 99–100, *101*, 102
information, applying 15–19

information processing speed 96, 97, 98–9
innovation 52, 125
intake forms 147, *148*, 149, *150–1*
inter-generational projects 140–1, *141*, *142*
interactive/ online galleries 161
interdependence 103
International Expressive Arts Therapy
    Association (IEATA) *159*
interpersonal communication 84
interpretation 80, *98*
intuition 49, *49*, 57, 58, 106, 122, 124
involuntary memories 27

joy 32, *32*, 45, 61, 132

K/ S (Kinesthetic/ Sensory) level of ETC
    creative behavior during 120–2, *122*,
        128–9, *128*
    directives 130, 133
    example of artwork 105, *106*
    in an holistic session 145
    and learning frameworks *109*, 111, *111*,
        112
    openings and closings to sessions 116–18,
        118
    rhythmic structure and versatility in
        directives 118–19
kinesthetics 29, 94
    see also K/ S

language disturbance, and cognitive
    impairment 88–9
language use 72–5
late-life creative self-expression and memory
    13–38
    Alzheimer's disease 20–1
    applying information 15–19
        overcoming ageism 17–18, *19*
    creativity for enhanced cognitive
        performance 14–15
    domains and artistic creativity *16*
    encouraging mental stimulation through
        expressive art-making 26–7
    goals *19*
    incorporating creativity into older adult
        identity through art-making 27–37
        creative behavior 29–31, *29*
        creative self-expression 35–7, *36*
        creative thought 31–5, *32*
    normal and abnormal aging 19, *20*
    risk factors of memory loss 21–4
        depression and social isolation 23–4
        mental stimulation 21–2
        stress 22–3
    self-expression in late-life 24–6
Latino culture 28, 62–3, 67–8, 103, 138, 154
learning

definition 103
ways to continue 161
Learning Evaluation Quiz 163–8
Likert scales *118*
limbic system 40, 92
lines
    cognition, mood and 56–7, *57*
    painting 119, 121, *122*
loneliness 18, 23, 24, 65
long-term memory 31, 93

mandalas 49, *49*, 50, *51*, 52, *123*, 124, 144
MCI (Mild Cognitive Impairment) 15, 20–1,
    23–4, 88
meaning, and symbolism *36*, 37
meaning-making 84
medical care, distrust of 138–9
meditation *48*, 55
Memories in the Making® 91
memory
    and cognitive impairment 92
    definition 103
    types 93–4
    verbal episodic 96, 97, 100–2, *101*, 102
memory functioning, understanding older
    adult self-perceived 157–8
memory loss, risk factors of 21–4
    depression and social isolation 23–4
    mental stimulation 21–2
    stress 22–3
memory techniques, expressivity-based 97–
    102, *98*, *101*
memory training, promoting socialization
    during 64–6
    see also cognitive training through creative
        self-expression
mental fatigue 110, 111
mental stimulation 21–2, 26–7
metamessages 73
metaphors 72, 73, 74–5, 77–8, 131
Mexican culture 67–8
Mild Cognitive Impairment *see* MCI
mind–body connections 48, *49*, 104, 107–8,
    130
Mini Mental Status Exam (MMSE) 153
mnemonic devices 96
modeling *29*, 30, 131
mood
    combining visual elements for enhanced
        58–61
        art-making in groups 59–61, *60*
    elevating during creative sessions 41–4, *42*
        bodily/ sensory pleasures 42–3, *42*
        gratifications 44
        higher order pleasures 43
    enhanced 84, 104, 105

making art that expresses and enhances 53–8
visual elements, cognition, and mood 54–8, *57*, *58*
motor coordination, and cognitive impairment 90–1
multicultural sensitivity 68
museums and galleries 129, 143, *146*
music, listening to 105, 119, *128*, 129

National Center for Creative Aging (NCCA) *159*, 160
NCCA (National Center for Creative Aging) 160
negotiated perspectives *36*, 37
nervous system, autonomous 86, 104, 108
neural confusion 75
neurobiology, of creativity and expressivity 102–3, *102*
neurological assessment *see* Clock Drawing Test
neurons
    firing 44–6, *45*
    loss of 20, 22, 23
    neurogenesis 22, 50, 51, 52
neuroplasticity 19, 51, 60, 103
neurotransmitters and creativity 46–7, 47–53
    acetylcholine 52–3, *53*
    dopamine 50–2, *51*
    neurotransmitters, brain waves, and memory training *48*
    serotonin 48–50, *49*
non-verbal communication 26, 67, 72–3

observation, and creative thought *32*, 34
one-to-one art therapy 152
openings, to art sessions 116–18, *118*
organic shapes 57
organizations 158–60, *159*
originality 25
overwhelmed, prevention of feeling 111, 118

P/ A (Perceptual/ Affective) level of ETC
    creative thought during 122–4, *123*, 126–8, *127*
    directives 131, 132–3
    example of artwork 105, *106*
    in an holistic session 145
    and learning frameworks *109*, 111, *111*, *112*
    rhythmic structure and versatility in directives 118–19
Parkinson's disease 88
pattern recognition *29*, 31, 97
perception 79, 91–2, *98*, 131
Perceptual/ Affective level of ETC *see* P/ A
persistence, and creative thought 32–3, *32*

personal interpretations 36, *36*
personal stories 24, 37, 43, 68, 86, 100–1, 106–7
physical activity *16*, 22
physical affection 69, 71
pink 75
plaques 20, 88
pleasures
    bodily 42–3, *42*, 48–50, *49*, 120–1
    higher order *42*, 43, 50, 99, 123
    rehabiliative 86
portrait painting process 32–3, 129–33
positive outcomes, rules that may promote 71–2
pragmatic competence 72, 73
predetermined session goals 114–15
procedural memory 93, 94, 120
processing, speed of 96, 97, 98–9

quadrants *60*
quilt-making 128–9, *128*
quiz 163–8

racism 62
reaction, and creative thought *32*, 34–5
reasoning 96, 97, *98*, 99–100, *101*, 102
red 54–6, 131
referral sheets 139
reinforcement *29*, 30, 67
relevance 86
reminiscence 43, 95–6, 131–2
repetition 48, *49*, 58, 86, 102, 111
resources and references 161
respect 26, 61, 62, 63, 70, 86, 134
response works 127–8, *127*
restorative strategies, in cognitive training 95–6
Rhyne's Visual Constructs Exercise 127, *127*
rhythmic intervals of stimulation 86, 118–19
Rorschach blots 42, *42*, 43, 94, 121–2, *122*
rules, that may promote positive outcomes with older adults 71–2

SAH (Society for Arts in Healthcare) *159*
saturation (color) 56
scope-of-practice 136–7
scribble drawings 105, 119, *128*, 129
self-care 24
self-criticism 109–10, *110*
self-discovery 25
self-esteem *49*
self-perceived memory functioning, understanding older adult 157–8
self-reflection 36, *36*
self-worth 17, 18, *19*, 24, 25–6
semantic memory 94
sensory experiences 27, 37

sensory pleasures *see* bodily pleasures
sensus communis 68
serotonin 48–50, *49*, 55, 56, 57, *57*, *58*, 59,
    121
sessions *see* art sessions
shape 57–8, *58*, 119
short-term memory 21, 31, 93, 126
single directive sessions 129–33
skilled nursing facilities 142, 145, *146*
small group format 114
social equality, vs. stratification during
    creativity and happiness 61–3
social inclusivity model 69, *69*
social isolation, and depression 23–4, 103
social sharing, of meaning through art 78–82
    evaluation and connection 81–2
    interpretation 80
    perception 79
socialization
    effects on 25, 53, 59, 60, 105, 130
    importance of 24, 137
    as part of an enriched environment 22
    promoting during memory training 64–6
Society for Arts in Healthcare (SAH) *159*
socio-economic factors 61–2, 72
space, cognition, mood and 57–8, *58*
Spanish culture *see* Hispanic culture
spirituality *16*, 126
spontaneity 49, 122
stand-alone training directives 129
standards, and creative thought *32*, 33
stimulation
    rhythmic intervals of 86, 118–19
    tapered 118, 126, 132
stratification, vs. social equality during
    creativity and happiness 61–3
stress 22–3, 34, 104, 128
stressors 152–3
symbiotic relationships 41
symbolism 26, 27, *36*, 37, 68, 74–5, 106
    see also C/ Sy
symptoms, identifying cross-culturally 152–8
    Clock Drawing Test 153–4, *154*, 156–7,
        157
    graphic indicators linked to cognitive
        impairment 156–7, *157*
    understanding older adult self-perceived
        memory functioning 157–8
synchronization, of bodily functions 104–5,
    108, 130

talk therapy 97
tangles 20, 88
tapered stimulation 118, 126, 132

therapeutic vs. educational frameworks, in
    cognitive training 108–12, *109*, *110*,
    111, *112*
timelines, for art sessions *116*
timing 30–1
transformational images 125–6, *125*
triadic schema 76, *76*, 104

universality 73

value (color) 56
varnish 133
venting 58–9
verbal associations 89
verbal episodic memory 96, 97, 100–2, *101*,
    102
versatility 118–19
violet 131
visual constructs exercise 127, *127*
Visual Conversation Activity 115, *115*, 141,
    142
visual elements, cognition, and mood 54–8
    color 54–6
    lines 56–7, *57*
    shape and space 57–8, *58*
visual literacy 77–8
visual search and identification 96, 97, 98–9,
    98, 101, *101*
Visual Thinking Strategies (VTS) 159–60, *159*
visualization 14, 36, 49, 98–9
visuospatial skills 89–90, *90*, 97, 131
voluntary memories 27
VTS (Visual Thinking Strategies) 159–60, *159*

warm colors 54–5, 131–2
webinars 160, 161
white 132
wisdom 24, 51–2, 126
working memory 93, 126

yellow 54–6, 132
yoga 117, 129, 144–5, *144*, *146*

AUTHOR INDEX

Aanstoos, J. 77
Abraham, R. 25
Administration on Aging 21, 139
Akdal, G. 89
Alba, R. 63
Albert, M. 110
Alberta, A. J. 138
Alders, A. 15, 22, 25, 28, 41, 43, 60, 62–3, 67, 68, 87, 92, 98, 105, 106–7, 109, 110, 111, 114, 115, 118, 120, 137, 138, 141, 145, 152, 153, 156
Alexander, T. 80
Alzheimer's Association 16, 19, 20, 21, 79, 88, 138, 139, 140, 152
American Psychological Association 19, 114
Anderson, T. 26, 36, 63, 66, 68, 70, 77, 79, 80, 81, 81–2, 97, 143
Andrade, J. 58
Angus, J. 17, 18
Aranda, M. P. 139, 140
Armstrong, K. 138
Arnheim, R. 77
Avison, W. R. 62
Azeemi, S. T. 55

Ball, K. 93, 95, 97, 114
Bang, M. 56, 57, 58
Bar-On, R. 64
Barron, A. 72, 73
Baune, B. 24
Becker, D. 100
Bergmen, H. 20–1, 40, 84
Berk, M. 138
Berleant, A. 27
Bermudez, D. 96
Berrios, G. 158
Berumen, L. C. 50, 51
Black, S. E. 90, 152, 153
Blanchard-Fields, F. 41
Boron, J. B. 99
Borrayo, E. A. 138, 139
Bracey, T. 31, 103
Bransford, J. D. 30
Braver, T. 23

Braverman, E. 46, 47
Bravo, M. 140
Brinck, I. 14
Brinkman, D. J. 84
Brochin-Ceballos, C. 68
Brown, A. L. 30
Butler, R. 43, 95
Butters, M. A. 16, 23, 24, 94

Caine, G. 22, 98
Caine, R. 22, 98
Calisch, A. 44
Campbell, R. L. 79, 100
Cann, A. 66
Carr, R. 91, 92, 94, 99, 100, 104–5
Carruthers, D. 31, 43
Carstensen, L. L. 40, 41
Chamberlain, A. 89
Chamorro-Premuzic, T. 103
Charles, S. T. 40, 41
Chauvin, B. 77
Chertkow, H. 20–1, 40, 84
Chow, J. C. 139
Chow, T. 66
Chudler, E. 46, 47
Chun, S.-I. 92
Claxton, A. F. 41
Cocking, R. R. 30
Cohen, G. 14, 68, 86–7, 102
Cole, M. G. 23
Comas-Dias, L. 67, 104
Connell, C. M. 138, 142
Corbie-Smith, G. 139
Cornwell, B. 65, 66
Cowan, P. 93, 94
Craig, D. 63
Cummings, J. L. 15, 88
Cummings, S. 24
Cunia, E. 29
Czeh, B. 21

Dahl, M. 72
Dalebroux, A. 58, 59
Davidson, R. J. 14, 40

De Petrillo, L. 27, 41, 88
Delahaye, B. L. 31, 32, 103
Dendukuri, N. 23
Depp, C. A. 18
Dewey, J. 70, 79, 81
Diamond, K. 17, 19
Diamond, M. 21, 22, 102
Dimond, M. 66
Dingfelder, S. 66
Dorn, C. M. 31, 103
Duzel, E. 51, 52

Ehrich, L. C. 31, 32, 103
Eisenberger, N. 18
Eisenberger, R. 29
Eknoyan, D. 156
Elias, J. W. 21, 90
Epstein, R. 14, 27, 89
Ertmer, P. A. 29

Fann, J. 84
Farbus, L. 23, 103
Felten, P. 78
Fisher, B. 27, 28
Franquiz, M. E. 68
Freedberg, D. 27, 78, 89
Furnham, A. 103
Fuster, J. M. 99

Gage, F. H. 22
Gallagher-Thompson, D. 95, 138, 140
Gallese, V. 27, 78, 89
Gallos, J. 76
Gast, D. 22
Gatz, M. 66
Gauthier, S. 20, 22, 23
Geary, J. 73, 75
Gilley, W. 23, 114
Glei, D. A. 14
Goldschmidt, G. 58
Goldstein, T. 58, 59
Grace, R. C. 30
Grady, C. L. 19, 21, 88
Graham, R. E. 28, 67
Gray, J. 23
Grealy, M. A. 23
Greaves, C. J. 23, 103
Grey, A. 60
Grier, E. C. 67
Gutierrez, K. D. 66, 103

Hannemann, B. T. 60, 103
Harlan, J. 87
Harris, M. 66, 72, 73, 80
Hass-Cohen, N. 91, 92, 94, 99, 100, 104, 104–5, 107–8
Helen, C. 83, 89

Hendrie, H. C. 85
Henley, D. 73, 74
Hevner, K. 56
Hinz, L. 105
Ho, L. 158
Hodges, H. F. 67
Horlings, R. 73, 92
Hou, C. E. 91
Howard, S. M. 88, 89
Huitt, W. 29, 30, 31

Islam, T. 63

Jameson, K. 67
Jeste, D. V. 14, 18
Jobe, J. B. 96
Jolley, R. P. 54
Jones, R. 66
Jung, R. E. 103

Kagin, S. L. 105
Kaplan, F. 87
Kasper, G. 72
Katon, W. 84
Keeley, A. C. 67
Kempermann, G. 22, 24, 103
Kim, M.-Y. 92
Kim, S.-H. 92
Kimura, S. 45
Kinney, J. M. 91
Kleiner-Fisman, G. 90, 152, 153
Kumaran, D. 51, 52

Labrecque, L. 54, 56
Lang, A. E. 90, 152, 153
Larrieu, S. 13
Laumann, E. O. 65
Lee, J.-H. 92
Leung, A. 68
Lichtenfeld, S. 55
Lieberman, M. 18
Liebmann, M. 115
Lindeman, R. 68–9, 70, 121, 139
Link, M. W. 97
Logsdon, R. G. 94, 120
Lopez, S. 152
Lu, L. 59
Lucassen, P. 21
Lusebrink, V. B. 37, 94, 104, 105, 107–8, 118, 120, 121, 122–3, 124

Mahoney, D. F. 67, 138
Malchiodi, C. 25, 44, 54, 56, 66, 76, 78, 100
Manly, J. J. 20, 88
Marder-Kamhi, M. 100
Martinez, D. 61
Mateer, C. A. 40, 85

Mather, M. 40, 41
Mattson, M. P. 22, 140
Maurer, K. 89, 152
McCurry, S. M. 94, 120
McGuigan, F. J. 107
McLaughlin, S. J. 138, 142
McNiff, S. 104
McSpadden, M. 58
Mehta, R. 54, 55, 55–6
Mell, J. C. 88, 89
Mendez, M. F. 15, 91
Merriam, S. B. 66
Messaris, P. 78
Metcafi, E. 68
MetLife Foundation 20
Milbrandt, M. 26, 36, 63, 66, 70, 77, 79, 80,
    81, 81–2, 97, 143
Miller, B. L. 88, 89, 91
Miller, D. B. 22, 22–3, 100
Milne, G. 54, 56
Minckler, D. 138
Mohamad, M. 66
Morano, C. L. 140
Morrell, M. 75, 76
Morris, C. B. 14
Mouton, C. 68–9, 70, 121, 139
Mungas, D. 14, 97
Musha, T. 45, 90, 152

Naiman, L. 15
Negash, S. 88
Neville, S. 17
Nevin, J. A. 30
Newby, T. J. 29

O'Callaghan, J. 22, 22–3, 100
O'Connell, M. E. 40, 85
O'Conner, R. C. 23
Ormrod, J. E. 29, 31
Ostbye, T. 23, 40
Østergaard, S. 25

Padilla, R. 83, 89
Pannells, T. C. 41
Paraiso, J. 63
Park, D. C. 96
Parks, A. 44
Pasupathi, M. 25
Pauwels, L. 77
Perneczky, R. 21
Perry, B. 85–6
Petersen, R. C. 88
Pittiglio, L. 95
Pizarro, J. 24
Potter, L. M. 23
Press, D. 94
Prior, S. 25

Pruessner, J. C. 23
Prvulovic, D. 89, 152

Radford, G. P. 80, 81
Radford, M. L. 80, 81
Raichle, M. 23
Rand, A. 27, 91
Rapp, R. 55, 75
Raza, M. 55
Reeve, P. 17, 18
Rentz, C. A. 91
Reynolds, F. 25
Rhyne, J. 127
Richards, M. 23, 84
Rodgers, W. 19
Rodin, J. 110
Rogoff, B. 66, 103
Ross, M. 25, 66
Rothman, S. M. 22, 140
Rubin, J. 100–1
Rush, J. 54, 56
Rusted, J. 87

Samton, J. 153
Sansone, C. 25
Sapolsky, R. 75
Sartwell, C. 68, 80
Schapiro, M. 54
Scheibe, S. 41
Schooler, J. W. 58
Schumm, L. P. 65
Schunk, D. H. 77, 84, 99, 102
Schur, C. 138
Schweitzer, L. 35
Scott Roberts, J. 138, 142
Seeman, T. E. 110
Seligman, M. E. P. 41, 43, 44
Serrano, C. 87, 153
Serrano, J. P. 95
Shanock, L. 29
Sheppard, L. 87
Silver, R. 22
Silvia, P. 87
Singer, T. 99
Sira, C. S. 40, 85
Sitzer, D. I. 14, 21, 94, 95, 96, 100, 114
Smallwood, J. 58
Snowdon, D. 87
Spendlove, D. 76
St. George, D. M. 139
Stankova, M. 72, 73
Steen, T. 44
Stephenson, M. 35
Stern, Y. 19, 40, 92
Stewart, E. G. 92
Studenski, S. 22

Stuhr, P. L. 14
Sunderland, T. 153
Sutcliffe, A. 65, 68, 69

Talamantes, M. 68–9, 70, 121, 139
ter Maat, M. 96
Teri, L. 94, 120
Thoman, D. 25, 103, 137
Thomas, D. R. 30
Thomas, G. V. 54
Thomas, S. B. 139
Thorsen, K. 66
Torrance, E. P. 84
Torres, L. 100
Triandis, H. C. 103
Tsai, A. Y. 23, 114
Tulving, E. 93, 100
Turner, R. J. 62
Twamley, E. W. 14

Ueda, Y. 55
Ueno, A. 98
University of California 21
Uotomoto, J. 84

Valentijn, S. A. M. 109–10
Van Gerven, P. 40, 98
Vanlierde, A. 14, 49, 91, 99
Verdugo, R. 61
Verret, L. 20–1, 40, 84
Vulchanov, V. 72, 73
Vulchanova, M. 72, 73

Wagle, A. 158
Wagster, M. V. 21, 90
Waller, D. 87
Wanet-Defalque, M.-C. 14, 49, 91, 99
Warga, M. 72, 73
Weisberg, R. 14
Weisman, A. 152
Welsch, W. 66
Whitbourne, S. 92
Williams, L. M. 41
Willis, S. L. 14, 95, 96, 98, 111
Wilson, A. 25, 66
Wilson, R. S. 65
Winner, E. 27, 41, 58, 59, 84, 88
Wood, A. H. 138
Woods, D. 95
Woolhiser-Stallings, J. 43, 95, 96, 97

Yamagami, T. 95
Ybarra, O. 65
Yener, G. 89
Yevin, I. 99
Yoto, A. 55

Zhu, R. J. 54, 55, 55–6
Zock, M. 55, 75